D0478815

KNITTING CLASSIC STYLE

35 MODERN DESIGNS INSPIRED BY FASHION'S ARCHIVES

VÉRONIK AVERY

Photographs by SARA CAMERON

STC CRAFT • A MELANIE FALICK BOOK • NEW YORK

IN MEMORY OF RENÉE SAINT–DENIS

Published in 2007 by Stewart, Tabori & Chang
An imprint of Harry N. Abrams, Inc.

Text copyright © 2007 by Véronik Avery
Photographs copyright © 2007 by Sara Cameron

All rights reserved. No portion of this book may be
reproduced, stored in a retrieval system, or
transmitted in any form or by any means, mechanical,
electronic, photocopying, recording, or otherwise,
without written permission from the publisher.

Library of Congress Cataloging-in-Publication Data:

Avery, Veronik.
    Knitting classic style : 35 modern designs
inspired by fashion's archives / by Veronik Avery ;
photographs by Sara Cameron.
        p. cm.
    Includes bibliographical references and index.
    ISBN-13: 978-1-58479-576-6
    ISBN-10: 1-58479-576-X
    1. Knitting--Patterns. I. Title.

TT820.A879 2007
746.43'2041--dc22   2006033120

Editor: Melanie Falick
Designer: Susi Oberhelman
Production Manager: Anet Sirna-Bruder

The text of this book was composed in
Estilo and Scala

Printed and bound in China
10 9 8 7 6 5 4 3 2 1

HNA
harry n. abrams, inc.
a subsidiary of La Martinière Groupe

115 West 18th Street
New York, NY 10011
www.hnabooks.com

CONTENTS

INTRODUCTION

You probably wouldn't know it from looking at me and my rather plain style of dress, but I adore fashion. Costume history, fashion photography, sociological and anthropological works—everything about fashion fascinates me. This interest may have started in childhood, when I followed my mother into boutiques and discovered how opinionated I could be; I was a child of the 1970s and, even at an early age, did not approve of the fashion of the times. The unfortunate pieced jean skirts and the ensemble of brown bell bottoms, turtleneck, and abbreviated pinafore I was forced to wear quickly shaped my fashion tastes and distastes. From early on, I've leaned toward an individual style of clothing—not exactly what is made available to the general public—so I learned how to sew and, eventually, how to knit in order to fulfill my "fashionable" pursuits.

I was a reluctant crafter; handicrafts weren't a tradition in my family, and I spent my high school years focusing on drama and photography, which led me to fine art photography after graduation. With the help of *Threads* magazine, I eventually taught myself to sew at nineteen, and through most of my twenties, which I spent pursuing a career as a costume designer, I maintained my post at the sewing machine. I quickly became as entranced in the process as in the end product—I enjoyed the entire experience, from drafting or fine-tuning a pattern to cutting out and sewing together the pieces. I loved the way it occupied my hands; while there was much to think through, the problems that arose had logical remedies, and my mind was often free to wander as I created.

During that time, I resisted knitting, thinking it would be too time-consuming. But in 2000, when my small daughter outgrew napping, leaving me with few uninterrupted blocks of time for sewing, I gave knitting a try and, as with sewing, taught myself. I found the world that welcomed me rich and varied, and almost immediately I was a goner. As with sewing, I began modifying patterns almost from the start, and it was a short leap from there to creating patterns of my own. I was especially excited about being able to create fabric and garment in one go—a novel concept to a dressmaker.

For me, both fashion and knitting serve a common purpose—the opportunity for creative, wearable self-expression—and it was in that spirit that I created this book.

Through most of the time I worked on it, I read solely about the subjects at hand—fashion and knitting. Together dress historians Anne Hollander and Philippe Perrot, sociologists Ted Polhemus and Ruth P. Rubinstein, and knitting historians Richard Rutt and Anne L. Macdonald informed my opinions in a way no single author could. I came to see an outfit as a visual representation, like a piece of art, while it may not carry the weight a work of art does, it still supports a range of points of view. An outfit is an expression of the individual wearing it, but at the same time, a viewer brings his or her own experiences—and thus his or her own meaning—to it. In her book *Dress Modes,* Ruth Rubinstein identifies many such layers of meaning—for example, meanings we might associate with styles based on cultural dress (such as a kimono) or clothing traditionally identified with a particular group or ideology (think military uniform or "preppie" style). In the end, it's almost impossible to understand a piece of clothing or a particular look as having one strict meaning; the layers of meaning that go into an outfit, into fashion, are many and personal, objective and subjective.

What I read confirmed something else I'd been surmising, but couldn't articulate: We live in interesting times insofar as our mode of dress is concerned. For our ancestors, clothing had little to do with choice and everything to do with what was available, affordable, and appropriate. The democratization of the last two centuries

or so—an equalizing of the classes brought about by the Industrial Revolution and World Wars, among other factors—allowed members of the middle class, for the first time, to dress as their wealthier counterparts, since they finally had money and opportunities once reserved for the very rich. The early 20th century was marked by a particular interest in fashion from Paris—it was common for western manufacturers to purchase Parisian *haute couture* models in order to copy them for the mass market, resulting in a sort of trickle-down effect. The wealthiest would wear the original designs, and cheaper and cheaper copies would become available as time went on, until basically everybody wore similar clothing, constructed to different quality standards.

This cycle continued until the 1960s, with fashion making subtle and logical evolutions every season and every year to keep factors such as skirt fullness and length, waist dimensions, and silhouettes ever-modern. But in recent decades, a shift has taken place in inspiration. Sometime in the late 1970s or early 1980s, fashion ceased to look forward in earnest and took to pillaging its archives instead. Fashion became about recalling a different time in history, and it did so consciously, reviving past fashions in a costume-like manner, such as Hollywood glamour in the seventies and Edwardian romanticism in the eighties. The result was greater flexibility; the conformity once demanded fell aside, allowing individuality and personal creativity to step forward.

Whether this is a postmodern phenomenon or simply a case of increased alternatives from a fashionable standpoint, the end result is the same. Divergent clothing styles are not only acceptable, they are desirable. It is ironic that although we are witnesses to an ever-increasing range of looks in magazines and higher-end ready-to-wear, most of us are faced with retail clothing stores that, out of reluctance to take risks on trends the general public may not embrace, offer the same basic uniform, subtly reworked from one season to the next. Fashion individualists find this stifling, so often use their own ingenuity to achieve a personalized look.

All of these factors place today's knitters in an advantageous position. They are able to create any style of their choosing, unhampered by rules regarding silhouette, color, or any other precept of fashion. A hard-earned finished product can be worn for any length of time. If the books published in recent years are any indication, knitters thrive on everything from quick knits to involved traditional creations—and in the current fashion climate, there is room for all.

For this book I aimed to encapsulate both modern and traditional standpoints by reinterpreting classics culled from four major themes—Fashion Mavens (women's wear), Tomboys (menswear), Global Travelers (ethnic costume), and Thrill Seekers (sportswear). I hope they will provide a backdrop for your unique vision as well.

As popular 1960s London designer Mary Quant once said, "Fashion, as we knew it, is over; people wear now exactly what they feel like wearing." I hope the following pages will inspire you to knit whatever it is you feel passionate about wearing.

The staples of classic feminine fashion often reference historical periods and can be rife with meaning—not only about a particular period, but also a woman's place within it. For example, Christian Dior's "New Look"—which emerged after World War II, when resources were scarce and women filled the workforce out of necessity—illustrates the layers of meaning that can be found within a simple outfit. Sensing that a "new look" was necessary to bolster postwar spirits, especially in Dior's heavily damaged France, he created a fresh and feminine fashion that rejected wartime frugality in favor of full skirts, luxurious fabrics, and dainty wasp-waists. The style served a postwar political agenda, too: Its very feminine silhouette idealized capable and lovely housewives, women whose skills, no longer needed in the workforce, were to be applied toward keeping a happy home. While lauded by the fashion cognoscenti of the time, the New Look was simultaneously scandalous for its extravagant use of fabric in the aftermath of World War II. Critics even suggested the designer was trying to undo women's advances by popularizing the corset again.

The following designs are my interpretations of pieces that have made an impact on women's fashion throughout history. The corset cover was necessitated by a very specific and important fashion staple, the corset, and the subsequent fashion emphasis on sculpting and restricting a woman's body. In the opposite spirit, the wrap styles of Claire McCardell (interpreted here in the Strawberry Lace Wrap Cardigan) and the comfortable fit and flattery of Madeleine Vionnet's bias-cut designs (Bias Shell) liberated women in a very physical way. The soft, close-fitting twinsets of the 1940s further emphasized the femininity of women in postwar times.

FASHION MAVENS

CORSET COVER

SIZES
X-Small (Small, Medium, Large, X-Large, 2X-Large)
Shown in size Small

FINISHED MEASUREMENTS
Chest: 32 (35, 38, 41¼, 44¼, 47¼)"

YARN
Reynolds Saucy (100% mercerized cotton; 185 yds / 100 g): 3 (3, 3, 4, 5, 6) balls #817 natural

NEEDLES
One 24" circular (circ) needle size US 6 (4mm)
Change needle size if necessary to obtain correct gauge.

NOTIONS
Waste yarn, stitch markers (one in contrasting color for beg of rnd), stitch holders, yarn needle

GAUGE
21 sts and 33 rows = 4" (10 cm) in Ric Rac Lace (see Chart)

STITCH PATTERN
Moss Stitch
(multiple of 2 sts; 4-rnd rep)
Rnds 1 and 2: [K1, p1] around.
Rnds 3 and 4: [P1, k1] around.
Rep Rnds 1–4 for Moss st.

NOTES
▸ Read the Body section of the pattern through before starting; patterning and shaping occur simultaneously.
▸ When working decreases in Moss st, if the 2nd st of the 2 being worked together is a knit st, k2tog; if 2nd st of 2 being worked together is a purl st, p2tog.

While some trends return once every generation, others reappear much more often. Victorian lingerie, like this corset cover, is an excellent example of a perennially popular style. Commonly known today as a shell, the corset cover was, from the 1860s on, a lightweight sleeved or sleeveless undergarment worn over the rigid, constraining corset to keep that expensive article of underclothing clean, provide warmth, and modestly cover the corset lest it show beneath the dress. The ribbons and lace used in these increasingly pretty and romantic garments, both fitted and unfitted, have contributed to their lasting appeal. While warmer than sewn covers, knit variations never attained the historical popularity of the former for one reason: They added to the circumference of a woman's waist.

Unlike its Victorian ancestors, my cover, designed to be worn solo or over another top in typical 21st-century fashion, is perfectly suited to the technique of knitting. The feminine detailing works up beautifully in mercerized cotton.

BODY
CO 168 (184, 200, 216, 232, 248) sts. Join for working in the rnd, being careful not to twist sts; place marker (pm) for beg of rnd.
Establish Border and Body Pattern: [Purl 1 rnd, knit 1 rnd] twice and on last rnd, mark 'side seam' by placing a second marker after 84 (92, 100, 108, 116, 124) sts. Beg with Rnd 2 of patt, work Moss st for 8 rnds. [Knit 1 rnd, purl 1 rnd] twice and on last rnd, place markers 11 sts before and after each marker.
Next rnd: *Work in Moss st to marker, slip marker (sm), work Row 1 of Ric Rac lace (see Chart) to next marker, sm, work in Moss st to side marker; rep from * once more. AT THE SAME TIME,
Shape Waist: When Body measures 1", dec 2 sts each side on next rnd, then every 4 rnds 6 times as follows: *K2tog (or p2tog), work in patt as est to 2 sts before side marker, k2tog (or p2tog); rep from * once more (see Notes)—70 (78, 86, 94, 102, 110) sts each Front and Back. Work even in patt as est until Body measures 5".
Shape Upper Body: Inc 2 sts each side on next row, then every 6 rnds 6 more times as follows: *K1, M1, work in patt as est to 1 st before side marker, M1, k1; rep from * once more—84 (92, 100, 108, 116, 124) sts each Front and Back. Work even until Body measures 10¼ (10½, 10¾, 11, 11¼, 11½)".
Divide for Armholes and Neck: BO 0 (2, 6, 6, 10, 14) sts, work 34 (36, 36, 40, 40, 40) sts in patt; place next 50 (54, 58, 62, 66, 70) sts on holder for right Front and last 84 (92, 100, 108, 116, 124) sts on 2nd holder for Back.

Shape Left Front Neck and Armholes:
Row 1 (WS): BO 8 sts, work in patt to end—26 (28, 28, 32, 32, 32) sts rem on Left Front.
Row 2 (RS): K1, k2tog, work in patt to end.
Row 3: BO 4 sts, work in patt to end.
Rep [Rows 2 and 3] 1 (1, 1, 2, 2, 2) more time(s)—16 (18, 18, 17, 17, 17) sts rem.
Next row: K1, k2tog, work in patt to end.
Next row: BO 3 sts, work in patt to end—12 (14, 14, 13, 13, 13) sts rem.
Cont decreasing at each RS armhole edge until 6 sts rem. Work even until strap measures 6½ (6¾, 7, 7¼, 7½, 7¾)". BO all sts.

Shape Right Front Neck and Armholes:
(RS) Slip last 34 (38, 42, 46, 50, 54) Front sts to needle, leaving 16 center Front sts on holder. Work 1 row in patt as est.
Row 1 (WS): BO 0 (2, 6, 6, 10, 14) sts, work in patt to end.
Row 2: BO 8 sts, work in patt to last 3 sts, ssk, k1.
Row 3 and all WS rows: Work in patt as est.
Row 4: BO 4 sts, work in patt to last 3 sts, ssk, k1.
Rep [Rows 3 and 4] 1 (1, 1, 2, 2, 2) more time(s)—16 (18, 18, 17, 17, 17) sts rem.
Work 1 WS row.
Next row (RS): BO 3 sts, work in patt to last 3 sts, ssk, k1.
Cont decreasing at each RS armhole edge until 6 sts rem. Work even until strap measures 6½ (6¾, 7, 7¼, 7½, 7¾)". BO all sts.

Shape Right Back Neck and Armholes:
(RS) Slip first 34 (38, 42, 46, 50, 54)
Back sts back to needle. BO 0 (2, 6, 6,
10, 14) sts, work 34 (36, 36, 40, 40, 40)
sts in patt. Work as for Left Front Neck
and Armholes.

Shape Left Back Neck and Armholes:
Work as for Right Front Neck and
Armholes.

FINISHING
Sew straps at shoulders.

Work Neck Edging: With RS facing
and beg at right shoulder, pick up and
knit 26 (28, 30, 32, 34, 36) sts along
strap, pm, 56 (56, 56, 64, 64, 64) sts
along Back Neck, pm, 52 (56, 60, 64,
68, 72) sts along left strap, pm, 56 (56,
56, 64, 64, 64) sts along Front Neck,
pm, 26 (28, 30, 32, 34, 36) sts along
strap, pm for beg   216 (224, 232, 256,
264, 272) sts. Purl 1 rnd.

Establish Neck Border:
Row 1: Knit to 1 st before 2nd marker,
turn;
Row 2: Yo, purl to first marker, turn;
Row 3: Yo, knit to yo from previous
row, k2tog (st before 2nd marker and
yo), knit to 1 st before 4th marker, turn;
Row 4: Yo, purl to 3rd marker, turn;
Row 5: Yo, knit to yo from previous
row, k2tog (st before 4th marker and
yo), knit to end.
Row 6: Purl to first marker, ssp (st after
marker and yo), purl to 4th marker, ssp
(st after marker and yo), purl to end.
Rep Rows 1–6 twice more. BO all sts.

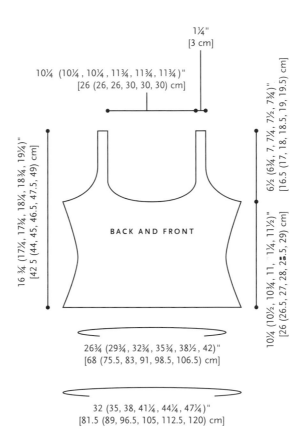

1¼"
[3 cm]

10¼ (10¼ , 10¼ , 11¾, 11¾, 11¾)"
[26 (26, 26, 30, 30, 30) cm]

6½ (6¾, 7, 7¼, 7½, 7¾)"
[16.5 (17, 18, 18.5, 19, 19.5) cm]

16 ¾ (17¼, 17¾, 18¼, 18¾, 19¼)"
[42 5 (44, 45, 46.5, 47.5, 49) cm]

BACK AND FRONT

10¼ (10¼, 10¾, 11, 11¼, 11½)"
[26 (26.5, 27, 28, 28.5, 29) cm]

26¾ (29¾, 32¾, 35¾, 38½, 42)"
[68 (75.5, 83, 91, 98.5, 106.5) cm]

32 (35, 38, 41¼, 44¼, 47¼)"
[81.5 (89, 96.5, 105, 112.5, 120) cm]

KEY

☐ Knit
⊡ Purl
⊙ Yo
⊠ P2tog
⊠ Ssp

RIC RAC LACE

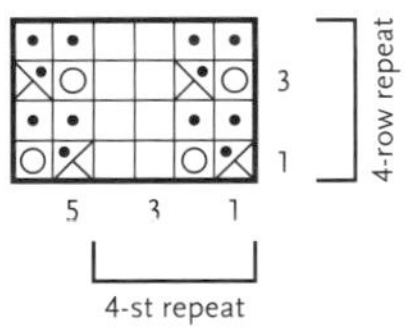

4-row repeat

5   3   1

4-st repeat

Armhole Edgings: (make 2)
With RS facing and beg at 'side seam,'
pick up and knit 2 (3, 7, 7, 11, 15) sts
along base of armhole, 70 (74, 78, 82, 86,
90) sts alongside strap, 2 (3, 7, 7, 11, 15)
sts along base of armhole—74 (80, 92, 96,
108, 120) sts. Pm for beg of rnd. Purl 1
rnd, knit 1 rnd, purl 1 rnd. BO all sts.

Weave in loose ends. Block to finished
measurements.

NOTE
▶ Work from right to left on all
rnds when working in-the-rnd.
▶ Work from right to left on RS
(odd-numbered) rows and
from left to right on WS rows
when working back and forth.

Bias Shell

SIZES
X-Small (Small, Medium, Large)
Shown in size Small

FINISHED MEASUREMENTS
Chest : 29½ (33, 36½, 40)"

YARN
Adrienne Vittadini Allegra (85%
cotton / 15% nylon; 87 yds / 50 g):
6 (6, 7, 8) balls #5014 black

NEEDLES
One 24" circular (circ) needle size
US 8 (5 mm)
One 24" circular needle size
US 7 (4.5 mm)
One set of five double-pointed
needles (dpn) size US 8 (5 mm)
One set of five double-pointed
needles size US 7 (4.5 mm)
Change needle size if necessary to
obtain correct gauge.

NOTIONS
Waste yarn, stitch markers (one in
contrasting color for beg of rnd),
stitch holders, yarn needle

GAUGE
19 sts and 24 rows = 4" (10 cm) in K1,
P2, K2, P2 Rib using larger needles

NOTES
▸ For best fit, select a size 3–4"
  (7.5–10 cm) smaller than actual
  bust measurement.
▸ Front and Back are identical. Each
  piece is begun by making a center-
  out ribbed square, worked in the
  round. The piece is then split at
  the neck and worked back and forth
  to the side seam. This seam and
  the armholes are shaped separately.

Nobody used fabric on the bias quite like Madeleine Vionnet, a near-mythic couturière at the cutting edge of Parisian fashion in the 1920s and 1930s. With it, she was able to design beautifully simple garments that showcased rather than molded the female form. This apparent simplicity was hard-won: In her book *Madeleine Vionnet,* costume historian Betty Kirke describes Vionnet's complex technique of tying weights to the fabric before sewing garments to eliminate the distortion associated with bias construction.

Knitwear doesn't have to be on the bias to move with our bodies, but the lines radiating from the center of a garment knit on the bias are flattering to many. Inspired by Vionnet, I designed this little black top, which is quick and easy to make. You begin by casting on a few stitches and working in the round from the center out until the finished width is attained; once this width has been reached, work continues one section at a time to lengthen the body and add the straps. No need to make a swatch first—just knit the back until it is about 6" square, block it with a shot of steam, and count your stitches. If your gauge is correct, keep going. If your gauge is off, simply begin again.

FRONT AND BACK

Using provisional method (see Special Techniques, page 136), waste yarn, and larger dpns, CO 8 sts. Distribute evenly on four needles; place marker (pm) for beg of rnd, and join, being careful not to twist sts. Knit 1 rnd.

Finally, the bottom portion is worked until the piece reaches desired length, after which the bottom corners are finished separately.
▸ Switch from dpns to circular needle when there are enough stitches to fit on the needle. Place markers to separate each dpn's section.

Begin Square:
Set-up Rnd 1: [K1, yo, k1] 4 times—12 sts.
Set-up Rnd 2: [K1, k1-tbl, k1] 4 times.
Set-up Rnd 3: [K1, yo, k1, yo, k1] 4 times—20 sts.
Set-up Rnds 4, 6, and 8: [K1, p1-tbl, work in patt as est to last 2 sts, end p1-tbl, k1] 4 times.
Set-up Rnd 5: [K1, yo, p1, k1, p1, yo, k1] 4 times—28 sts.
Set-up Rnd 7: [K1, yo, p2, k1, p2, yo, k1] 4 times—36 sts.
Continue with Rib Pattern:
Rnd 1: [K1, yo, k1, work in patt as est to last 2 sts on needle, k1, yo, k1] 4 times—44 sts.
Rnd 2: Rep Set-up Rnd 4.
Rnd 3: [K1, yo, k1, work in patt as est to last 2 sts on needle, k1, yo, k1] 4 times—52 sts.

Rnd 5: [K1, yo, p1, work in patt as est to last 2 sts on needle, p1, yo, k1] 4 times—60 sts.

Rnd 7: [K1, yo, p1, work in patt as est to last 2 sts on needle, p1, yo, k1] 4 times—68 sts.

Rnd 9: [K1, yo, k1, work in patt as est to last 2 sts on needle, k1, yo, k1] 4 times—76 sts.

Rnd 11: [K1, yo, p1, work in patt as est to last 2 sts on needle, p1, yo, k1] 4 times—84 sts.

Rnd 13: [K1, yo, p1, work in patt as est to last 2 sts on needle, p1, yo, k1] 4 times—92 sts.

Rep Rnds 1–7 (1–9, 1–11, 1–13)—124 (132, 140, 148) sts, switching to circ needle when possible and placing markers on circ needle to define each dpn section (see Notes). Cont working increases before and after markers on odd rounds as before.

Divide for Neck: Remove beg-of-rnd marker, turn.

Next row (WS): *P1, k1-tbl, work in patt to 2 sts before next marker, k1-tbl, p1, sm; rep from * to end. Turn.

Next row (RS): Work in patt to 1 st before marker, yo, k1, sm, [k1, yo, work in patt to 1 st before next marker, yo, k1, sm] twice, k1, yo, work in patt to end—6 sts inc'd. Cont in this manner, working back and forth, increasing 1 st on each side of marker and working new sts in rib patt until there are 178 (198, 218, 238) sts on needle—40 (44, 48, 52) on either side of neckline and 49 (55, 61, 67) on each lower quadrant.

Upper Right Seam Edge:

Row 1 (RS): Work in patt to last 3 sts before first marker, k2tog, k1, turn. Place rem sts on 2 separate holders (upper left section on one holder and two bottom sections on second holder)—39 (43, 47, 51) sts rem.

Row 2: Work in patt as est.

Rep [Rows 1–2] 4 (6, 8, 10) more times, and Row 1 once more—34 (36, 38, 40) sts rem.

Shape Right Armhole: BO 16 (18, 20, 22) sts at beg of next row—18 sts rem. BO 2 sts at beg of every following WS row until 4 sts rem. Work 1 row, then BO 4 rem sts.

Upper Left Seam Edge: Slip 40 (44, 48, 52) upper left section sts back to needle.

Row 1 (RS): K1, ssk, work in patt to end.

Row 2: Work in patt as est.

Rep [Rows 1–2] 5 (7, 9, 11) more times—34 (36, 38, 40) sts rem.

Shape Left Armhole: BO 16 (18, 20, 22) sts at beg of next RS row—18 sts rem. BO 2 sts at beg of every following RS row until 4 sts rem. Work 1 row, then BO 4 rem sts.

Shape Bottom: Slip 98 (110, 122, 134) bottom section sts back to needle.

Row 1 (RS): K1, ssk, work in patt to 1 st before center marker, yo, k1, sm, k1, yo, work in patt to last 3 sts, k2tog, k1.

Row 2: Work in patt to 2 sts before center marker, k1-tbl, p1, sm, p1, k1-tbl, work in patt to end.

Rep Rows 1–2 until bottom section measures 8¾ (9¼, 9¾, 10½)" or desired length from horizontal line, ending with a WS row.

Shape Bottom Right Corner:

Row 1 (RS): K1, ssk, work in patt to last 3 sts before center marker, k2tog, k1. Place rem sts on holder for bottom left corner.

Row 2: Work in patt as est.

Rep Rows 1 and 2 until 4 sts rem. Cut yarn, thread through rem sts, and pull tight.

Shape Bottom Left Corner: Slip bottom left sts back to needle, and work as for right corner.

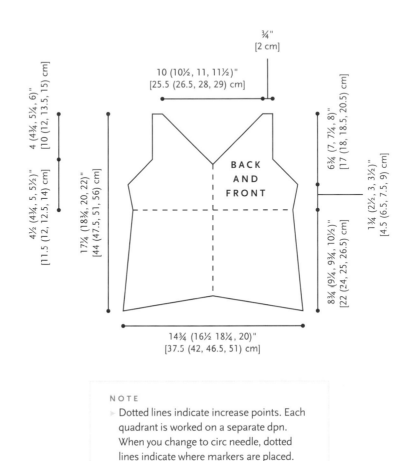

3/4"
[2 cm]

10 (10½, 11, 11½)"
[25.5 26.5, 28, 29) cm]

4 (4¾, 5¼, 6)"
[10 (12, 13.5, 15) cm]

4½ (4¾, 5, 5½)"
[11.5 (12 12.5, 14) cm]

17¼ (18¾, 20, 22)"
[44 (47.5, 51, 56) cm]

BACK
AND
FRONT

6¾ (7, 7¼, 8)"
[17 (18, 18.5, 20.5) cm]

1¾ (2½, 3, 3½)"
[4.5 (6.5, 7.5, 9) cm]

8¾ (9¼, 9¾, 10½)"
[22 (24, 25, 26.5) cm]

14¾ (16½ 18¼, 20)"
[37.5 (42, 46.5, 51) cm]

NOTE

▷ Dotted lines indicate increase points. Each quadrant is worked on a separate dpn. When you change to circ needle, dotted lines indicate where markers are placed.

FINISHING

Sew shoulders and side seams.

Armhole Edgings: (RS) Using smaller dpns, pick up and knit 64 (68, 72, 76) sts evenly around armhole. Purl 1 rnd. Work 2 rnds of K2, P2 Rib. Loosely BO all sts.

Neck Edging: (RS) Using smaller circ needle, pick up and knit 33 (37, 43, 47) sts along each side of neckline—132 (148, 172, 188) sts. Purl 1 rnd. Work 2 rnds of K2, P2 Rib. Loosely BO all sts.

Bottom Edging: (RS) Using smaller circ needle, pick up and knit 66 (76, 86, 96) sts each along Front and Back—132 (152, 172, 192) total sts. Work 4 rnds of K2, P2 Rib. Loosely BO all sts.

Thread tail from CO onto yarn needle and run though base of CO sts. Remove waste yarn and pull tail tight. Weave in loose ends. Block to finished measurements.

SILK PURSE

FINISHED MEASUREMENTS
Circumference: 9½"
Length: 6¼"

YARN
Adrienne Vittadini Celia (100% silk; 109 yds / 25 g): 1 ball #900 brown

NEEDLES
One set of five double-pointed needles (dpn) size US 0 (2mm) Change needle size if necessary to obtain correct gauge.

NOTIONS
Stitch markers (one in contrasting color for beg of rnd), yarn needle

GAUGE
32 sts and 44 rnds = 4" (10 cm) in Stockinette stitch (St st)

STITCH PATTERN
Trinity Stitch
(multiple of 4 sts; 4-rnd rep)
Rnds 1 and 3: Purl.
Rnd 2: *(K1, p1, k1) in one stitch, p3tog; rep from * around.
Rnd 4: *P3tog, (k1, p1, k1) in one stitch; rep from * around.
Rep Rnds 1–4 for Trinity St.

Throughout history, knitting crazes have come and gone—the 1930s' argyle sock fever, the colorful British intarsia sweaters of the 1980s, the recent scarf trend. In the late 18th and early 19th centuries, the rage was for coin purses crafted by knitting or netting, a technique in which yarn is knotted to form a network of regularly spaced stitches. Women liked to make these popular accessories for themselves or as gifts for gentlemen. While wool, linen, and cotton were all used at the time, silk was the preferred fiber. Also fashionable were misers' purses—long, tubular purses with a lengthwise slit in the middle, folded to create two sacks carried at the fold. Both styles were also crocheted; they were often made in metallic thread and embellished with beads.

While knit on small needles, this purse, modeled after the netted coin purse, is still a quick project—and one that I enjoy for its jewel-like appearance. Since many of us would consider it too small to be truly useful, I've imagined it as a ball holder, for fashionable knitting on the go.

PURSE

Bottom: CO 6 sts. Distribute evenly on three needles; place marker (pm) for beg of rnd and join for working in the round, being careful not to twist sts.
Rnds 1 and 3: Knit.
Rnd 2: K1, M1, k2, M1, k2, M1, k1—9 sts.
Rnd 4: K3, M1, k3, M1, k3, M1—12 sts.
Rnd 5: [K2, pm] around.
Rnd 6: [K1, M1, knit to next marker] around—18 sts.
Rep Rnd 6 every other rnd until there are 13 sts between each marker—78 sts. Knit 1 rnd even.
Inc rnd: [P39, M1] twice—80 sts. Knit 1 rnd, redistributing sts on four needles (20 sts each). Purl 3 rnds.
Make Ridge: *Knit next st together with st 4 rnds below (last knit rnd); rep from * across.

Begin Pattern: Work Rnds 1–4 of Trinity st 7 times—purse measures approx 5". Purl 4 rnds. Make a second ridge in same manner as the one preceding Trinity st. Knit 2 rnds.
Eyelets: [K2, k2tog, yo] around. Knit 4 rnds. Work 2 Garter ridges (knit 1 rnd, purl 1 rnd). BO all sts.

FINISHING
With yarn doubled, make two 14" twisted cords (see Special Techniques, page 136). Using yarn needle, thread through eyelets separately so that tied ends are at opposite ends and cords weave alternately though eyelets.

Weave in loose ends. Block to finished measurements.

Strawberry Lace Wrap Cardigan

SIZES
X-Small (Small, Medium, Large, X-Large, 2X-Large)
Shown in size Medium

FINISHED MEASUREMENTS
Chest: 35 (38¾, 42¼, 45¾, 49¾, 52¾)"

YARN
Reynolds Odyssey (100% merino wool; 104 yds / 50 g): 13 (14, 16, 17, 19, 20) balls #505 red mix

NEEDLES
One 32" circular (circ) needle size US 5 (3.75 mm)
One pair straight needles size US 6 (4 mm)
Change needle size if necessary to obtain correct gauge.

NOTIONS
Waste yarn, stitch markers, stitch holders, yarn needle, medium-sized crochet hook

GAUGE
18 sts and 26 rows = 4" (10 cm) in Strawberry Lace using larger needles

STITCH PATTERN
Strawberry Lace
(multiple of 8 sts + 3; 12-row rep)
Row 1: *Yo, [slip 1, k2tog, psso], yo, k5; rep from * to last 3 sts before marker, end yo, [slip1, k2tog, psso], yo.
Row 2 and all WS rows: Purl.
Row 3: *K1, yo, ssk, k5; rep from * to last 3 sts before marker, end k1, yo, ssk.
Row 5: Knit.
Row 7: *K4, yo, [slip 1, k2tog, psso], k1; rep from * to last 3 sts before marker, end k3.
Row 9: *K5, yo, ssk, k1; rep from * to last 3 sts before marker, end k3.
Row 11: Knit.
Row 12: Purl.
Rep Rows 1–12 for Strawberry Lace.

NOTE
▸ If fewer than 2 sts precede or follow a yarnover as a result of shaping, work these sts in St st.

Wrapped tops and dresses became an integral part of modern American fashion largely because of the comfort and ease of wearing they brought to American women, long used to conforming their bodies to rigid, constricting styles. As early as World War II, designer Claire McCardell began selling the wildly successful Popover, a belted, wrap-front dress made in a variety of utilitarian fabrics such as denim and wool jersey. Diane Von Furstenberg then took the fashion world by storm in 1972 with her justly famous wrap dress, which she still sells.

Like these wrap garments, my cardigan boasts comfort and elegance, as well as the advantage of fitting a variety of figures. Reminiscent of the sweaters worn by dancers during rehearsal—when ease and movement are so important—it's knit with two-ply, tone-on-tone variegated yarn, which adds richness and depth to its straightforward construction.

BACK
Hem: With waste yarn, smaller needles, and using provisional method (see Special Techniques, page 136), CO 81 (89, 97, 105, 113, 121) sts. Beg with a RS row, work 10 rows of St st. Purl 1 row (turning row). Change to larger needles and work in St st for 11 more rows.

Establish Pattern: (RS) K3, place marker (pm), work Row 1 of Strawberry Lace over next 75 (83, 91, 99, 107, 115) sts, pm, k3. Work even until piece measures 19½ (19¾, 20, 20¼, 20½, 20¾)" from the turning row, ending with a WS row.
Shape Armholes: (RS) BO 3 (4, 5, 6, 7, 8) sts at beg of next 2 rows. Dec 1 st at each edge on next row (see Note), then every other row 4 (5, 6, 7, 8, 9) more times as follows: K2, k2tog, knit to last 4 sts in patt as est, ssk, k2—65 (69, 73, 77, 81, 85) sts rem. Work even until armhole measures 7¼ (7½, 7¾, 8, 8¼, 8½)". Place rem sts on holder.

LEFT FRONT
Hem: With waste yarn, smaller needles, and using provisional method, CO 69 (73, 77, 81, 85, 89) sts. Beg with a RS row, work 10 rows of St st. Purl 1 row (turning row). Change to larger needles and work in St st for 11 more rows.

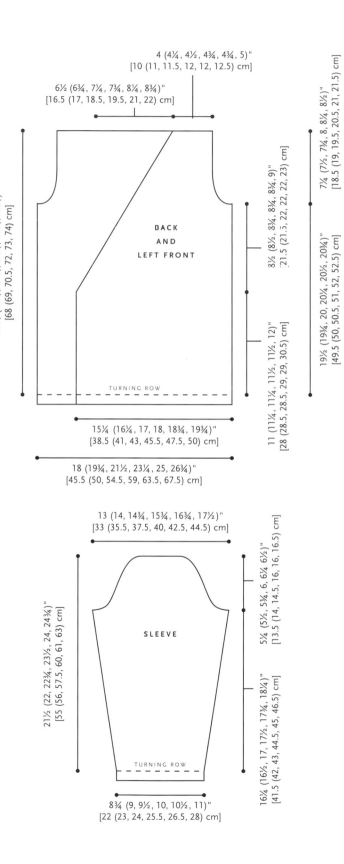

4 (4¼, 4½, 4¾, 4¾, 5)"
[10 (11, 11.5, 12, 12, 12.5) cm]

6½ (6¾, 7¼, 7¾, 8¼, 8¾)"
[16.5 (17, 18.5, 19.5, 21, 22) cm]

7¼ (7½, 7¾, 8, 8¼, 8½)"
[18.5 (19, 19.5, 20.5, 21, 21.5) cm]

26¾ (28¼, 27¾, 28¼, 28¾, 29¼)"
[68 (69, 70.5, 72, 73, 74) cm]

BACK
AND
LEFT FRONT

8½ (8½, 8¾, 8¾, 8¾, 9)"
21.5 (21.5, 22, 22, 22, 23) cm]

19½ (19¾, 20, 20¼, 20½, 20¾)"
[49.5 (50, 50.5, 51, 52, 52.5) cm]

11 (11¼, 11¼, 11½, 11½, 12)"
[28 (28.5, 28.5, 29, 29, 30.5) cm]

TURNING ROW

15¼ (16¼, 17, 18, 18¾, 19¾)"
[38.5 (41, 43, 45.5, 47.5, 50) cm]

18 (19¾, 21½, 23¼, 25, 26¾)"
[45.5 (50, 54.5, 59, 63.5, 67.5) cm]

13 (14, 14¾, 15¾, 16¾, 17½)"
[33 (35.5, 37.5, 40, 42.5, 44.5) cm]

5¼ (5½, 5¾, 6, 6¼, 6½)"
[13.5 (14, 14.5, 16, 16, 16.5) cm]

21½ (22, 22¾, 23½, 24, 24¾)"
[55 (56, 57.5, 60, 61, 63) cm]

SLEEVE

16¼ (16½, 17, 17½, 17¾, 18¼)"
[41.5 (42, 43, 44.5, 45, 46.5) cm]

TURNING ROW

8¾ (9, 9½, 10, 10½, 11)"
[22 (23, 24, 25.5, 26.5, 28) cm]

Establish Pattern: (RS) K5 (3, 5, 3, 5, 3), pm, work Row 1 of Strawberry Lace over next 59 (67, 67, 75, 75, 83) sts, pm, k5 (3, 5, 3, 5, 3). Cont in patt as est until piece measures 11 (11¼, 11¼, 11½, 11½, 12)" from turning row, ending with a WS row.

Note: Neck and armhole shaping are worked concurrently in the next section; please read pattern all the way through before continuing.

Shape Neck: (RS) Dec 1 st at neck edge on next row, then every other row as follows: Work in patt as est to last 4 sts, ssk, k2 (see Note). Cont working in this manner until piece measures 19½ (19¾, 20, 20¼, 20½, 20¾)" from the turning row, ending with a WS row.
Shape Armhole and Continue Neck Shaping: (RS) BO 3 (4, 5, 6, 7, 8) sts, work to last 4 sts, ssk, k2. Dec 1 st at armhole and neck edges on next row, then every other row 4 (5, 6, 7, 8, 9) more times as follows: K2, k2tog, work in patt to last 4 sts, ssk, k2— 5 (6, 7, 8, 9, 10) sts dec'd at armhole. Maintaining patt as est, cont to dec 1 st at neck edge every other row until 18 (19, 20, 21, 22, 23) sts rem on needle. Work even until armhole measures 7¼ (7½, 7¾, 8, 8¼, 8½)". Place rem sts on holder.

RIGHT FRONT
Hem: With waste yarn, smaller needles, and using provisional method, CO 69 (73, 77, 81, 85, 89) sts. Beg with a knit row and work 10 rows of St st. Purl 1 row (turning row). Change to larger needles and work in St st for 11 more rows.
Establish Pattern: (RS) K5 (3, 5, 3, 5, 3), pm, work Row 1 of Strawberry Lace patt over next 59 (67, 67, 75, 75, 83) sts, pm, knit to end. Cont in patt as est until piece measures 11 (11¼, 11¼,

11½, 11½, 12)" from turning row, ending with a WS row.

Note: Neck and armhole shaping are worked concurrently in the next section; please read pattern all the way through before continuing.

Shape Neck: (RS) Dec 1 st at neck edge on next row, then every other row as follows: K2, k2tog (see Note), work in patt to end. Cont working in this manner until piece measures 19½ (19¾, 20, 20¼, 20½, 20¾)" from the turning row, ending with a RS row.
Shape Armholes and Continue Neck Shaping: (WS) BO 3 (4, 5, 6, 7, 8) sts at beg of next row. Dec 1 st at armhole and neck edges on next row, then every other row 4 (5, 6, 7, 8, 9) more times as follows: K2, k2tog, work in patt to last 4 sts, ssk, k2—5 (6, 7, 8, 9, 10) sts dec'd at armhole. Maintaining patt as est, cont to dec 1 st at neck edge every other row until 18 (19, 20, 21, 22, 23) sts rem on needle. Work even until armhole measures 7¼ (7½, 7¾, 8, 8¼, 8½)". Place rem sts on holder.

SLEEVES (make 2)
Hem: With waste yarn, smaller straight needles, and using provisional method, CO 39 (41, 43, 45, 47, 49) sts. Beg with a RS row, work 10 rows in St st. Purl 1 row (turning row). Change to larger needles. Work in St st for 11 more rows.
Establish Pattern: (RS) K2 (3, 4, 5, 2, 3), pm, work Row 1 of Strawberry Lace over next 35 (35, 35, 35, 43, 43) sts, pm, k2 (3, 4, 5, 2, 3). Cont in patt as est until piece measures 3" from turning row, ending with a WS row.
Shape Sleeve: (RS) Inc 1 st each side on next row, then every 8 rows 9 (10, 8, 7, 5, 3) times, and every 6 rows 0 (0, 3, 5, 8, 11) times as follows: K2, M1-R, work in patt as est to last 2 sts, M1-L, k2—59 (63, 67, 71, 75, 79) sts. Work

even until piece measures 16¼ (16½, 17, 17½, 17¾, 18¼)" from the turning row, ending with a WS row.
Shape Caps: (RS) BO 3 (4, 5, 6, 7, 8) sts at beg of next 2 rows. Dec 1 st each side on next row, then every other row 16 (17, 18, 19, 20, 21) more times as follows: K2, k2tog, work in patt to last 4 sts, ssk, k2—19 sts rem. BO all sts.

FINISHING
Join Shoulders: With RS held together and starting at shoulder edge, join 18 (19, 20, 21, 22, 23) shoulder sts using the 3-needle BO method (see Special Techniques, page 136). Rep for other side—29 (31, 33, 35, 37, 39) sts rem for Back neck.

Sew sleeves into armholes. Sew side and sleeve seams. Fold hems to wrong side and whipstitch live sts into place.

BAND
With circ needle, RS facing, and beg at bottom of right Front, pick up and knit 118 (120, 122, 124, 126, 128) sts along right Front edge, 29 (31, 33, 35, 37, 39) sts along Back neck, and 118 (120, 122, 124, 126, 128) sts along left Front edge—265 (271, 277, 283, 289, 295) sts. Knit 2 rows. BO all sts loosely.

BELT
With smaller straight needles, CO 6 sts. Work in Garter stitch for 48". BO all sts.

BELT LOOPS
Try on sweater to find natural waist. Mark waist position at each side. Using crochet hook, make 1 single crochet just above marked position and 10 chain sts. Make 1 more sc just below marked position. Cut yarn and pull through.

Weave in loose ends. Block to finished measurements.

Woolen Cashmere Twinset

SIZES
Small (Medium/Large, X-Large, 2X-Large)
Shown in size Small

FINISHED MEASUREMENTS
Chest: 35¼ (41, 46¾, 52½)" (closed)

YARN
Lana Gatto VIP (80% wool / 20% cashmere; 218 yds / 50 g): 9 (10, 11, 13) balls #10054 pink

NEEDLES
One 36" circular (circ) needle size US 2 (2.75 mm)
One 36" circular needle size US 3 (3.25 mm)
One pair straight needles size US 2 (2.75 mm)
One pair straight needles size US 3 (3.25 mm)
Change needle size if necessary to obtain correct gauge.

NOTIONS
Cable needle (cn), stitch holders, size C/2 (2.75 mm) crochet hook, yarn needle, thirteen ⁷⁄₁₆" shank buttons

GAUGE
36 sts and 48 rows = 4" (10 cm) in cable pattern (see Chart A) using larger needles

STITCH PATTERN
Mini-Cable Rib
(multiple of 4 sts + 6; 2-row rep)
Row 1 (WS): P1, k1, *p2, k2; rep from * to last 4 sts, p2, k1, p1.
Row 2: K1, p1, *RT, p2; rep from * to last 4 sts, RT, p1, k1.
Rep Rows 1 and 2 for Mini-Cable Rib.

ABBREVIATIONS
RT (Right Twist): Skip first st and knit into 2nd st, then knit into skipped st; slip both sts from needle together.
Dec2-back: Slip 2 sts to cable needle (cn) and hold cn parallel to and behind left needle. *Insert right needle into first st on left needle and first st on cn, knit these 2 sts tog; rep from * once—2 sts decreased.
Dec2-front: Slip 2 sts to cn and hold cn parallel to and in front of the left needle. *Insert right needle into first st on cn and first st on left needle, knit these 2 sts tog; rep from * once—2 sts decreased.

NOTES
▷ This project is worked back and forth; a circular needle is required to accommodate the large number of sts.
▷ Work edge stitches in St st.
▷ After working armhole decs on Fronts and Back, work rem 3 sts of 6-st cable at armhole edge as a 3-st cable.

The classic twinset first appeared in the 1940s—a very feminine sweater and cardigan set made of wool or cashmere. The traditional version is round-necked, with a short-sleeved sweater and long-sleeved cardigan, worn unbuttoned. Stars such as Marilyn Monroe helped popularize the tight-fitting sweater set, which women often wore with pearls.

Breaking away from the classical model, I had a bit of fun playing up the T-shirt look of the turtleneck underneath by adding an image to the front. I considered all kinds of figures, but eventually opted for a decorative ornament that recalls both a strand of yarn and an infinity symbol. As a variation, you can knit this model using an ornament of your own choice, by sketching it or printing it from your computer onto knitter's graph paper. Once your design has been transferred to the special paper at the appropriate gauge, use a pencil to fill in the stitches.

Cardigan

BODY
Rib: Using smaller circ needle, CO 294 (342, 390, 438) sts. Work Mini-Cable Rib for 2½", ending with a RS row.
Set-up row (WS): P1 (edge st), k1, *p1, M1P, p1, k2, p6, k2; rep from * to last 4 sts, p1, M1P, p1, k1, p1 (edge st)—319 (371, 423, 475) sts. Change to larger circ needles.
Establish Cable Pattern: (RS) K1 (edge st), p1, work Row 1 of Chart A to last 2 sts, end p1, k1 (edge st). Work even in patt as est until Body measures 14¼ (15, 15¾, 16½)", ending with a WS row.
Divide for Fronts and Back: (RS) Maintaining patt as est, work 75 (79, 96, 100) sts for Right Front and place on holder; BO 13 (24, 23, 34) sts; work 143 (165, 185, 207) sts for Back and place on holder; BO 13 (24, 23, 34) sts; work to end.

LEFT FRONT

Shape Armhole: (WS) Maintaining patt as est, work 1 row.

Next row (RS): BO 5 (7, 9, 11) sts, work to end.

Work 1 row. Dec 2 sts at armhole edge on next row, then every 4 rows 2 (3, 4, 5) times as follows: K1, p1, Dec2-back (see Notes), work to end—64 (64, 77, 77) sts rem. Work even until armhole measures 4 (4¼, 4¾, 5¼)", ending with a WS row.

Shape Neck: (RS) Work to last 10 (10, 12, 12) sts and place these on holder without working them.

Row 1 (WS): P1, k1, k2tog, work in patt as est to end.

Row 2: Work in patt to last 4 sts, p2tog, p1, k1.

Rep these 2 rows 5 (5, 7, 7) more times, then work Row 2 every RS row 12 times—30 (30, 37, 37) sts rem. Work even until piece measures 7¾ (8½, 9¼, 10)" from armhole. Place all sts on holders.

BACK

Shape Armholes: (WS) Slip Back sts on holder back to needle and attach yarn. Maintaining patt as est, work 1 row. BO 5 (7, 9, 11) sts at beg of next 2 rows. Dec 2 sts at each armhole edge on next row, then every 4 rows 2 (3, 4, 5) times as follows: K1, p1, Dec2-back, knit to last 6 sts, Dec2-front, p1, k1—121 (135, 147, 161) sts rem.

Next RS row: Work even to last 2 sts, end p2tog 0 (1, 0, 1) time(s)—121 (134, 147, 160) sts rem. Work even until Back measures same as left Front to shoulder. Place all sts on holder.

RIGHT FRONT

Shape Armhole: (WS) Slip Right Front sts on holder back to needle and attach yarn. Maintaining patt as est, work 2 rows.

Next row (WS): BO 5 (7, 9, 11) sts at beg of row. Dec 2 sts at armhole edge on next row, then every 4 rows 2 (3, 4, 5) times as follows: Work in patt to last 6 sts, Dec2-front, p1, k1—64 (64, 77, 77) sts rem. Work even until armhole measures 4 (4¼, 4¾, 5¼)", ending with a RS row.

Shape Neck: (WS) Work in patt to last 10 (10, 12, 12) sts and place these on holder without working them.

Row 1 (RS): K1, p1, ssp, work to end.

Row 2: Work to last 4 sts, ssk, k1, p1.

Rep these 2 rows 5 (5, 7, 7) more times, then work Row 1 every RS row 12 times—30 (30, 37, 37) sts rem. Work even until right Front measures same as left Front to shoulder. Place all sts on holders.

SLEEVES (make 2)

Cuff: With smaller needles, CO 70 (82, 94, 106) sts.

Next row (RS): K1 (edge st), p1, *k2, p2; rep from * to last 4 sts, k2, p1, k1 (edge st). Work Mini-Cable Rib for 2", ending with a RS row.

Set-up row (WS): P1, k1, *p6, k2, p1, M1P, p1, k2; rep from * to last 8 sts, end p6, k1, p1—75 (88, 101, 114) sts.

Establish Cable Pattern: (RS) Change to larger needles. K1 (edge st), p1, work Row 1 of Chart B to last 2 sts, k1 (edge st).

Shape Sleeve: (RS) Inc 1 st each end every 8 rows 15 times as follows: K1, p1, M1P, work in patt as est to last 2 sts, M1P, p1, k1, working all new sts in rev St st—105 (118, 131, 144) sts. Work even until Sleeve measures 12½ (12¾, 13¼, 13¾)" from beg, or desired length, ending with a WS row.

Shape Cap: (RS) BO 3 (5, 6, 7) sts at beg of next two rows, then BO 5 (7, 8, 9) sts at beg of following 2 rows—89 (94, 103, 112) sts rem. Dec 2 sts each side on next row, then every 4 rows 5 times, every 6 rows 3 (5, 7, 8) times, then every 4 rows 5 (3, 2, 2) times as follows: K1, p1, Dec2-back, work in patt as est to last 6 sts, Dec2-front, p1, k1—33 (38, 43, 48) sts rem. BO 3 (4, 4, 5) sts at beg of next 2 rows—27 (30, 35, 38) sts rem. BO all sts.

FINISHING

Join shoulders (working from armhole to neck on each side) using the 3-needle BO method (see Special Techniques, page 136)—61 (74, 73, 86) Back neck sts rem.

LEFT BUTTON BAND

(RS) With smaller needles, pick up and knit 211 (219, 227, 235) sts along left Front edge. Knit 2 rows.

Establish Rib:

Row 1 (WS): Slip 1, k1, *p2, k2; rep from * to last st, end p1.

Row 2: K1, p2, *RT, p2; rep from * to last 4 sts, RT, p1, k1.

Cont in Mini-Cable Rib as est for 5 more rows. BO in rib.

RIGHT BUTTONHOLE BAND

(RS) With smaller needles, pick up and knit 211 (219, 227, 235) sts along right Front edge. Knit 2 rows.

Establish Rib:

Row 1 (WS): P1, *k2, p2; rep from * to last 2 sts, end k2.

Row 2: Slip 1, p1, *RT, p2; rep from * to last 4 sts, RT, p2, k1.

Rep Row 1 once more.

Buttonhole Row: (RS) Work 16 (20, 24, 28) sts in patt as est, *yo, p2tog, work 14 sts in patt as est; rep from * 11 times, yo, p2tog, work in patt to end. Cont in Mini-Cable Rib as est for 3 more rows. BO in rib.

COLLAR BAND

(RS) With smaller needles, pick up and knit 52 (54, 62, 64) sts along right Front neck, knit up 61 (74, 73, 86) Back neck sts on holder, pick up and knit 53 (54, 63, 64) sts along left Front neck—166 (182, 198, 214) sts. Knit 2 rows.

Establish Rib:

Row 1 (WS): *P2, k2: rep from * to last 2 sts, end p2.

Row 2: *RT, p2; rep from * to last 2 sts, RT. Rep Row 1, then BO all sts in rib.

Top Button Loop: Using crochet hook and beg at top right corner, make 1 single crochet into band corner and 6 chain sts. Make 1 more sc into top Garter ridge. Cut yarn and pull through.

Block to finished measurements. Sew sleeves into armholes. Sew side and sleeve seams. Sew on buttons opposite buttonholes and button loop. Weave in loose ends.

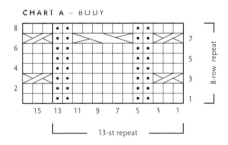

CHART A – BODY

8-row repeat

13-st repeat

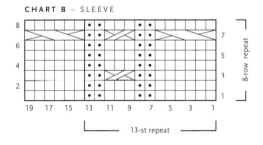

CHART B – SLEEVE

8-row repeat

13-st repeat

KEY

 Knit on RS, purl on WS.

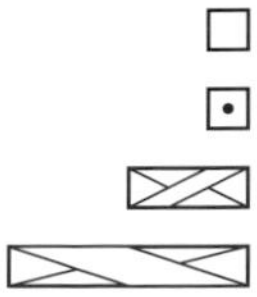

Purl on RS, knit on WS.

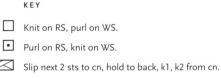 Slip next 2 sts to cn, hold to back, k1, k2 from cn.

Slip next 3 sts to cn, hold to back, k3, k3 from cn.

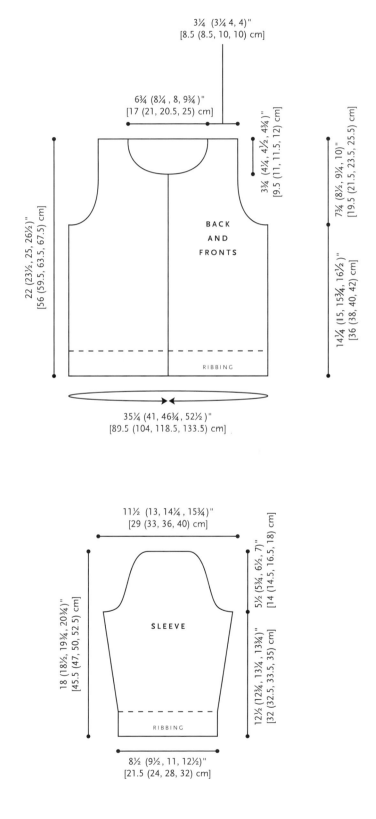

3¼ (3¼ 4, 4)"
[8.5 (8.5, 10, 10) cm]

6¾ (8¼ , 8, 9¾)"
[17 (21, 20.5, 25) cm]

3¾ (4¼, 4½, 4¾)"
[9.5 (11, 11.5, 12) cm]

7¾ (8½, 9¼, 10)"
[19.5 (21.5, 23.5, 25.5) cm]

BACK AND FRONTS

14¼ (15, 15¾, 16½)"
[36 (38, 40, 42) cm]

22 (23½, 25, 26½)"
[56 (59.5, 63.5, 67.5) cm]

RIBBING

35¼ (41, 46¾, 52½)"
[89.5 (104, 118.5, 133.5) cm]

11½ (13, 14¼, 15¾)"
[29 (33, 36, 40) cm]

5½ (5¾, 6½, 7)"
[14 (14.5, 16.5, 18) cm]

SLEEVE

18 (18½, 19¾, 20¾)"
[45.5 (47, 50, 52.5) cm]

12½ (12¾, 13¼, 13¾)"
[32 (32.5, 33.5, 35) cm]

RIBBING

8½ (9½, 11, 12½)"
[21.5 (24, 28, 32) cm]

Short-sleeved Turtleneck

SIZES
X-Small (Small, Medium, Large, X-Large,
2X-Large, 3X-Large)
Shown in size Small

FINISHED MEASUREMENTS
Bust: 31 (34, 37½, 41, 46, 47½, 51)"

YARN
Lana Gatto VIP (80% wool / 20%
cashmere; 218 yds /50 g): 8 (9, 10, 11,
13, 13, 14) balls #10054 pink (MC); 1 (1,
2, 2, 2, 2, 2) ball(s) #12504 gray (CC)

NEEDLES
One pair straight needles size
US 3 (3.25 mm)
One pair straight needles size
US 2 (2.75 mm)
One 16" circular (circ) needle size
US 2 (2.75 mm)
Change needle size if necessary to
obtain correct gauge.

NOTIONS
Stitch holders, markers, bobbins
(optional for Intarsia), yarn needle,
cable needle (cn)

GAUGE
29 sts and 43 rows = 4" (10 cm) in
Stockinette stitch (St st) on larger needles

STITCH PATTERNS
Mini-Cable Rib
(multiple of 4 sts + 6; 2-row rep)
Row 1 (WS): P1 (edge st), k1, *p2,
k2; rep from * to last 4 sts, p2, k1, p1
(edge st).
Row 2: K1 (edge st), p1, *RT, p2; rep
from * to last 4 sts, RT, p1, k1 (edge st).
Rep Rows 1 and 2 for Mini-Cable Rib.

Twisted Rib (multiple of 2 sts; 1-rnd rep)
Rnd 1: [K1-tbl, p1-tbl] around.
Rep Rnd 1 for Twisted Rib.

BACK

Rib: Using smaller needles, CO 122 (134, 146, 158, 170, 182, 194) sts. Work in Mini-Cable Rib for 1½", ending with a RS row. Change to larger needles and beg St st. Purl 1 row.

Shape Waist: (RS) Dec 1 st at each edge on next row, then every 4 rows 11 times as follows: K1, ssk, knit to last 3 sts, k2tog, k1—98 (110, 122, 134, 146, 158, 170) sts rem. Work 10 rows even. Inc 1 st each edge on next row, then every 8 rows 7 times as follows: K2, M1-R, knit to last 2 sts, M1-L, k2—114 (126, 138, 150, 162, 174, 186) sts. Work even until piece measures 13¼ (13½, 13¾, 14, 14¼, 14½, 14¾)", ending with a WS row.

ABBREVIATIONS
RT (Right Twist): Skip first st and knit 2nd
st, then knit skipped st; slip both sts from
needle together.
Dec2-back: Slip 2 sts to cable needle (cn)
and hold cn parallel to and behind left
needle. * Insert right needle into first st
on left needle and first st on cn, knit
these 2 sts tog; rep from * once —2 sts
decreased.
Dec2-front: Slip 2 sts onto cn and hold cn
parallel to and in front of the left needle.
*Insert right needle into first st on cn and
first st on left needle, knit these 2 sts tog;
rep from * once—2 sts decreased.

NOTES
▸ Work all edge stitches in St st.
▸ Work Color Chart using Intarsia method.
  Use bobbins or separate lengths of yarn
  for each section of chart; do not be
  tempted to work stranded technique
  across smaller areas—it will affect your
  tension and show on the RS.

Shape Armholes: (RS) BO 2 (3, 3, 4, 4, 5, 5) sts at beg of next 2 rows, and 2 (2, 3, 3, 4, 4, 5) sts at beg of following 2 rows—106 (116, 126, 136, 146, 156, 166) sts rem. Dec 2 sts at each edge on next row, then every 4 rows 2 (3, 4, 5, 7, 8, 9) times, and every 8 rows 1 (1, 1, 1, 0, 0, 0) time(s) as follows: K2, Dec2-back, knit to last 6 sts, Dec2-front, k2—90 (96, 102, 108, 114, 120, 126) sts rem. Work even until armholes measure 5½ (5¾, 6, 6¼, 6¼, 6½, 6¾)", ending with a WS row.

Shape Shoulders and Back Neck: (RS) BO 6 (3, 5, 7, 4, 6, 3) sts, k22 (27, 27, 27, 32, 32, 35), join a second ball of yarn and k34 (36, 38, 40, 42, 44, 50), then place these sts on holder for back neck, knit to end of row.

Next row: BO 6 (3, 5, 7, 4, 6, 3) sts for left shoulder, purl to end of row—22 (27, 27, 27, 32, 32, 35) sts rem each shoulder. Working on both sides at the same time, BO 4 (5, 5, 5, 6, 6, 7) sts at shoulder edges 5 times and, AT THE SAME TIME, dec 1 st at each neck edge twice as follows: Work to 4 sts before neck edge, ssk, k2; k2, k2tog, knit to end of row—0 sts rem.

FRONT

Work as for Back until piece measures 7¾ (8, 8¼, 8½, 8¾, 9, 9¼)", ending with a WS row. Mark center 47 sts.

Establish Intarsia Pattern: (RS) Knit to marker and begin Chart. Work 89 rows of Chart, working waist and armhole shaping as for Back. Remove markers when Chart is complete. Work even until armholes measure 3 (3¼, 3½, 3¾, 3¾, 4, 4¼)", ending with a WS row.

Shape Neck: (RS) K40 (42, 44, 46, 48, 50, 52), join a second ball of yarn and k10 (12, 14, 16, 18, 20, 22), then place

these sts on holder for Front neck,
knit to end of row. BO 2 sts at each neck
edge 4 times, then BO 1 st at neck edge
every RS row 6 times—26 (28, 30, 32, 34,
36, 38) sts rem each shoulder. Work even
until armholes measure 5½ (5¾, 6, 6¼,
6¼, 6½, 6¾)", ending with a WS row.
Shape Shoulders: (RS) BO 6 (3, 5, 7, 4,
6, 3) sts at each shoulder edge once,
then BO 4 (5, 5, 5, 6, 6, 7) sts at shoulder
edges 5 times—0 sts rem.

SLEEVES (makes 2)
With smaller needles, CO 86 (90, 98,
102, 110, 114, 118) sts. Work in Mini-

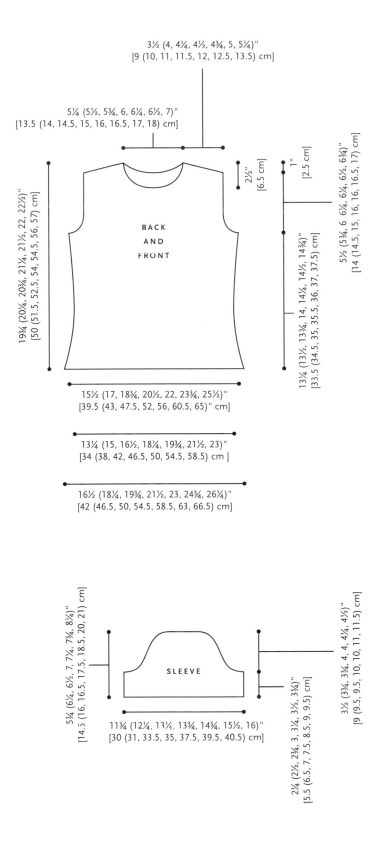

3½ (4, 4¼, 4½, 4¾, 5, 5¼)"
[9 (10, 11, 11.5, 12, 12.5, 13.5) cm]

5¼ (5½, 5¾, 6, 6¼, 6½, 7)"
[13.5 (14, 14.5, 15, 16, 16.5, 17, 18) cm]

2½"
[6.5 cm]

1"
[2.5 cm]

BACK
AND
FRONT

5½ (5¾, 6, 6¼, 6¼, 6½, 6¾)"
[14 (14.5, 15, 16, 16.5, 17) cm]

19¾ (20¼, 20¾, 21¼, 21½, 22, 22½)"
[50 (51.5, 52.5, 54, 54.5, 56, 57) cm]

13¼ (13½, 13¾, 14, 14¼, 14½, 14¾)"
[33.5 (34.5, 35, 35.5, 36, 37, 37.5) cm]

15½ (17, 18¾, 20½, 22, 23¾, 25½)"
[39.5 (43, 47.5, 52, 56, 60.5, 65)" cm]

13¼ (15, 16½, 18¼, 19¾, 21½, 23)"
[34 (38, 42, 46.5, 50, 54.5, 58.5) cm]

16½ (18¼, 19¾, 21½, 23, 24¾, 26¼)"
[42 (46.5, 50, 54.5, 58.5, 63, 66.5) cm]

SLEEVE

3½ (3¾, 3¾, 4, 4, 4¼, 4½)"
[9 (9.5, 9.5, 10, 10, 11, 11.5) cm]

5¾ (6¼, 6½, 7, 7¼, 7¾, 8¼)"
[14.5 (16, 16.5, 17.5, 18.5, 20, 21) cm]

2¼ (2½, 2¾, 3, 3¼, 3½, 3¾)"
[5.5 (6.5, 7, 7.5, 8.5, 9, 9.5) cm]

11¾ (12¼, 13¼, 13¾, 14¾, 15½, 16)"
[30 (31, 33.5, 35, 37.5, 39.5, 40.5) cm]

Cable Rib for ¾", ending with a RS row. Change to larger needles. Beg with a WS row, work even in St st for 1½ (1¾, 2, 2¼, 2½, 2¾, 3)", ending with a WS row.

Shape Cap: (RS) BO 2 (3, 3, 4, 4, 5, 5) sts at beg of next 2 rows and 2 (2, 3, 3, 4, 4, 5) sts at beg of following 2 rows—78 (80, 86, 88, 94, 96, 98) sts rem. Dec 2 sts at each edge on next row, then every other row 2 (3, 3, 3, 4, 3, 3) times, every 4 rows 2 (2, 1, 2, 1, 2, 3) time(s), every 6 rows 1 (2, 2, 2, 2, 2, 2) time(s), every 4 rows 3 (3, 2, 2, 2, 2, 2) times, and every other row 2 (2, 4, 5, 5, 6, 5) times as follows: K1, p1, Dec2-back, knit to last 6 sts, Dec2-front, p1, k1—34 (32, 34, 32, 34, 32, 34) sts rem. BO 4 (3, 4, 3, 4, 3, 4) sts at beg of next 2 rows—26 sts rem. BO all sts.

FINISHING

Sew shoulder seams.

Collar: (RS) With smaller circ needle, pick up and knit 62 (64, 66, 68, 70, 72, 74) sts along Front neck and 50 (52, 54, 56, 58, 60, 62) sts along Back neck—112 (116, 120, 124, 128, 132, 136) sts. Pm for beg of rnd and join. Purl 2 rnds.

Rib: Work in Twisted Rib for 4¼".

Stripe Pattern: Cont in Twisted Rib, working stripe pattern as follows: 1 rnd CC, 2 rnds MC, 2 rnds CC, 2 rnds MC, 1 rnd CC. With CC, BO loosely in Rib.

Sew sleeves into armholes. Sew side and sleeve seams. Weave in loose ends. Block to finished measurements.

KEY

☐ Knit on RS, purl on WS.
☐ MC
■ CC

INTARSIA CHART

LITTLE GIRL'S A-LINE JACKET

SIZES
Children's size 2 (4, 6, 8)
Shown in size 6

FINISHED MEASUREMENTS
Chest: 22 (27, 29, 36)" (closed)

YARN
Muench Tessin (43% superwash new
wool / 35% acrylic / 22% cotton; 110
yds / 100 g): 6 (7, 9, 12) balls #801
white/primary

NEEDLES
One 24" circular (circ) needle
size US 7 (4.5 mm)
One set of five double-pointed
needles (dpn) size US 7 (4.5 mm)
Change needle size if necessary to
obtain correct gauge.

NOTIONS
Stitch holders, stitch markers, yarn
needle, 6 (7, 8, 8) [⅝"] buttons, small
amount of fiberfill

GAUGE
18 sts and 24 rows = 4" (10 cm) in
Stockinette stitch (St st)

NOTE
▶ This project is worked back and
forth; a circular needle is required
to accommodate the large number
of stitches.

In creating this hooded cardigan, I chose a cape-like A-line silhouette, a traditional style for babies and small children that is particularly flattering for little girls. It is also loosely based on the matinee jacket, a short and sweet knitted day coat popular for babies in the early 20th century that was traditionally decorated with lace patterns and ribbon.

The inspiration for the decorative elements on my version came from a completely different source: the colorful designs in Anna Zilboorg's *45 Fine and Fanciful Hats to Knit*. In the book, Anna tops her hats with little knitted balls instead of pompoms and offers a pattern for a hat adorned with several bobbles. With a playful, decorative theme in mind, I styled a jacket for my princess complete with swing, texture, and an elfin hood.

BODY
CO 149 (173, 197, 229) sts.
*Row 1 (WS): Knit.
Row 2: K1, M1-R, knit to last stitch, M1-L, k1—151 (175, 199, 231) sts. Rep from * once more—153 (177, 201, 233) sts. Knit 1 row.
Begin Border Pattern: (RS) K6, work Row 1 of Chart as given for your size to last 6 sts, k6. Maintaining first and last 6 sts in Garter stitch, work Rows 2–8 of Chart.
Establish Body Pattern:
Row 1 (RS): Knit.
Row 2: K6, *p9 (11, 9, 11), k3; rep from * to last 15 (17, 15, 17) sts, p9 (11, 9, 11), k6. Rep Rows 1 and 2 until piece measures 3½ (3½, 4, 4¼)" from beg, ending with a WS row.
First Decrease Row: (RS) K6, *k2tog, k5 (7, 5, 7), ssk, k3; rep from * to last 3 sts, k3—129 (153, 169, 201) sts. Work even in patt as est until piece measures 4½ (4½, 4½, 4¾)" from beg, ending with a WS row.
Make Buttonhole: (RS) K2, BO 4 sts, knit to end. On return row, CO 4 sts

over bound-off sts of previous row. AT THE SAME TIME, make buttonhole every 12 rows 5 (6, 7, 8) more times. Cont in patt as est until piece measures 7 (7, 8, 8½)", ending with a WS row.
Second Decrease Row: (RS) K6, *k2tog, k3 (5, 3, 5), ssk, k3; rep from * to last 3 sts, k3—105 (129, 137, 169) sts. Cont in patt as est until piece measures 10¼ (10¾, 12¼, 12¾)", ending with a WS row.
Divide for Fronts and Back: (RS) K29 (35, 37, 45) sts and place on holder for right Front, k1, M1, k45 (57, 61, 77), M1, k1 and place on second holder for Back, knit to end.

LEFT FRONT
(WS) Cont on left Front only, work even until armhole measures 4¾ (6¼, 6¾, 8¼)". Place all sts on holder.

BACK
(WS) Slip 49 (61, 65, 81) Back sts from holder to needle, and work even in patt as est until armholes measure 4¾ (6¼, 6¾, 8¼)". Place all sts on holder.

14), pick up and knit 1 st at right shoulder seam, k15 (19, 15, 19), pick up and knit 1 st at left shoulder seam, knit to end—41 (49, 41, 49) sts. Work even in patt as est until Hood measures 1½ (1½, 1, 1)", ending with a RS row.

Shape Hood: (WS) K6, *pm, k5 (7, 5, 7), pm, k3; rep from * 3 more times, end k3. Inc 8 sts on next row, then every 10 (10, 8, 8) rows 4 (4, 6, 6) more times as follows: K6, *slip marker (sm), M1-R, knit to next marker, M1-L, sm, knit to next marker; rep from * 3 more times, sm, k6—81 (89, 97, 105) sts. Work even until Hood measures 8½ (9, 9½, 10)". Turn inside out and fold in half. Join at top using 3-needle BO method.

SLEEVES (make 2)

Cuff: CO 32 (32, 38, 38) sts. Knit 6 rows.

Begin Border Pattern: (RS) K3, work Row 1 of Chart as given for your size to last 2 sts, k2. Maintaining first 3 sts and last 2 sts in Garter st, work Rows 2–8 of Chart. Purl 1 row.

Reverse for Cuff and Establish Sleeve Pattern: (was WS, now RS) K3, [pm, p7 (7, 9, 9), pm, k3] twice, pm, p7 (7, 9, 9), pm, end k2. Work even in patt as est until piece measures 6 (5, 5, 4)" from beg, ending with a WS row.

Shape Sleeve: (RS) Inc 6 sts on next row, then every 22 (16, 16, 10) rows 1 (3, 3, 5) more time(s) as follows: K3, [sm, M1-R, knit to next marker, M1-L, sm, knit to next marker] 3 times, sm, k2—44 (56, 62, 74) sts. Work even until Sleeve measures 10¼ (11¾, 14½, 14¾)" from cuff turn or desired length. BO all sts.

FINISHING

With a 10" yarn strand, make a twisted cord (see Special Techniques, page 136).

RIGHT FRONT

(WS) Slip 29 (35, 37, 45) right Front sts from holder to needle, and work even in patt as est until armhole measures 4¾ (6¼, 6¾, 8¼)". Place all sts on holder.

JOIN SHOULDERS

With RS held together and starting at shoulder edge, join 17 (21, 25, 31) shoulder sts using 3-needle BO method (see Special Techniques, page 136). Rep for other side—39 (47, 39, 47) neck sts rem.

HOOD

Slip 39 (47, 39, 47) neck sts from holder to needle. With RS facing and beg at right Front edge, k12 (14, 12,

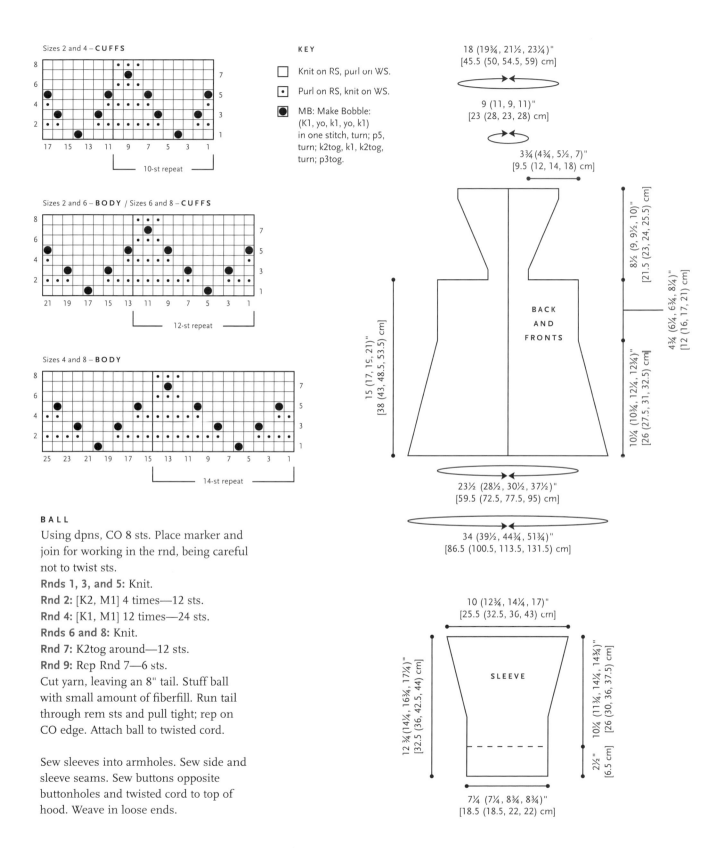

Sizes 2 and 4 – **CUFFS**

8
6
4
2
7
5
3
1
17 15 13 11 9 7 5 3 1

— 10-st repeat —

Sizes 2 and 6 – **BODY** / Sizes 6 and 8 – **CUFFS**

8
6
4
2
7
5
3
1
21 19 17 15 13 11 9 7 5 3 1

— 12-st repeat —

Sizes 4 and 8 – **BODY**

8
6
4
2
7
5
3
1
25 23 21 19 17 15 13 11 9 7 5 3 1

— 14-st repeat —

KEY

☐ Knit on RS, purl on WS.

⊡ Purl on RS, knit on WS.

◉ MB: Make Bobble:
(K1, yo, k1, yo, k1)
in one stitch, turn; p5,
turn; k2tog, k1, k2tog,
turn; p3tog.

BALL

Using dpns, CO 8 sts. Place marker and join for working in the rnd, being careful not to twist sts.

Rnds 1, 3, and 5: Knit.

Rnd 2: [K2, M1] 4 times—12 sts.

Rnd 4: [K1, M1] 12 times—24 sts.

Rnds 6 and 8: Knit.

Rnd 7: K2tog around—12 sts.

Rnd 9: Rep Rnd 7—6 sts.

Cut yarn, leaving an 8" tail. Stuff ball with small amount of fiberfill. Run tail through rem sts and pull tight; rep on CO edge. Attach ball to twisted cord.

Sew sleeves into armholes. Sew side and sleeve seams. Sew buttons opposite buttonholes and twisted cord to top of hood. Weave in loose ends.

18 (19¾, 21½, 23¼)"
[45.5 (50, 54.5, 59) cm]

9 (11, 9, 11)"
[23 (28, 23, 28) cm]

3¾ (4¾, 5½, 7)"
[9.5 (12, 14, 18) cm]

8½ (9, 9½, 10)"
[21.5 (23, 24, 25.5) cm]

4¾ (6¼, 6¾, 8¼)"
[12 (16, 17, 21) cm]

BACK
AND
FRONTS

15 (17, 19, 21)"
[38 (43, 48.5, 53.5) cm]

10¼ (10¾, 12¼, 12¾)"
[26 (27.5, 31, 32.5) cm]

23½ (28½, 30½, 37½)"
[59.5 (72.5, 77.5, 95) cm]

34 (39½, 44¾, 51¾)"
[86.5 (100.5, 113.5, 131.5) cm]

10 (12¾, 14¼, 17)"
[25.5 (32.5, 36, 43) cm]

SLEEVE

12¾ (14¼, 16¾, 17¼)"
[32.5 (36, 42.5, 44) cm]

10¼ (11¾, 14¼, 14¾)"
[26 (30, 36, 37.5) cm]

2½"
[6.5 cm]

7¼ (7¼, 8¾, 8¾)"
[18.5 (18.5, 22, 22) cm]

Basque Beret

YARN
Grignasco Cashmere (100%
cashmere; 240 yds / 25 g): 2 balls
#564 navy

NEEDLES
One 16" circular (circ) needle size
US 3 (3.25 mm)
One 16" circular needle size
US 0 (2 mm)
One set of five double-pointed (dpn)
needles size US 3 (3.25 mm)
Change needle size if necessary to
obtain correct gauge.

NOTIONS
Waste yarn, stitch markers (one in
contrasting color for beg of rnd),
yarn needle

GAUGE
24 sts and 32 rnds = 4" (10 cm) in
Checkerboard Stitch using larger
needles

STITCH PATTERN

Checkerboard Stitch
(multiple of 4 sts; 4-rnd rep)
Rnds 1 and 2: [K2, p2] around.
Rnds 3 and 4: [P2, k2] around.
Rep Rnds 1–4 for Checkerboard Stitch.

NOTES
▸ Decrease in pattern as follows: if the
2nd stitch is a knit stitch, ssk; if the
2nd st is a purl stitch, ssp.
▸ Change to dpn when the work no
longer fits on the circ needle.

Few items of clothing have been laden with such visual significance as the beret. Part of the military uniform of the French alpine armed units and the American Special Forces, it has been the stereotypical garb of Frenchmen, beatniks, and film directors, and is also frequently donned by boy scouts, revolutionaries, and elegant women. The practical nature of the beret explains its broad appeal: Cheap and easy to make, the beret is flattering to most people and can be rolled up and stuffed in a pocket when no longer needed. The beret is similar to the Scottish tam, but smaller and less floppy, with no pompom.

I modeled the shape of this cap after the first berets, which originated in the northern Basque country of France. The Basque people knit their berets in sheep's wool, but I opted for a soft cashmere yarn instead.

BERET

Brim: Using provisional method (see Special Techniques, page 136) and larger circ needle, CO 100 sts. Place marker (pm) for beg of rnd and join, being careful not to twist sts. Knit 8 rnds. Using smaller circ needle, pick up live sts from cast-on rnd. Fold brim up so that rev St st is visible on the outside, holding needles parallel to one another. Join the sts on both needles as follows: *Knit together 1 st from smaller needle and 1 st from larger needle; rep from * around. Set smaller needle aside.

Body:
Rnd 1: [P2, M1] around—150 sts.
Rnd 2: [P75, M1] twice—152 sts.
Work even in Checkerboard st until Beret measures 6¾" from beg.
Next rnd: Remove marker, k1, replace marker for new beg of rnd, [work 26

sts in patt as est, pm] 4 times, work 24 sts in patt as est, pm, work 24 sts in patt as est.

Decrease for Top:
Rnds 1 and 2: [Slip marker (sm), ssk (or ssp; see Notes), work in patt as est to next marker] 4 times, work in patt to end of rnd—144 sts.
Rnd 3: [Sm, ssk (or ssp), work in patt as est to next marker] 6 times—138 sts. Cont decreasing as in Rnd 3 until 6 sts rem.

FINISHING

Tip of Beret: K2tog, knit to end of rnd. Transfer rem sts to 1 dpn, and work I-cord (see Special Techniques, page 136) for ½". Cut yarn, leaving an 8" (20.5 cm) tail. Thread though rem sts and pull tight.

Weave in loose ends. Block to finished measurements.

It's curious to me how many people regard menswear as uninteresting—
at least compared to women's wear—when, in actuality, icons of male
fashion such as British aristocrats, fishermen, and soldiers continually
inspire designers of women's clothing. There is something to be said
for the sheer practicality of menswear, and while woolen suits and
sweaters were once solely in the domain of menswear, many women
appear all the more feminine when clad in a simple woolen outfit.

An early attempt to incorporate menswear into women's
wardrobes was made by London's Rational Dress Society in 1881, driven
by the radical idea that women should have to wear no more than seven
pounds of underwear (fourteen was typical), and should not deform
their bodies for fashion. They promoted bloomers—light, baggy trousers
worn under the skirt—which eventually became acceptable as cycling
attire, but did not immediately find a place in the fashion mainstream.
In the 1920s and 1930s, Gabrielle Chanel popularized practical clothes
for women—including pants and boxy jackets made from comfortable
fabrics—and the masculine influence took off. Katherine Hepburn's
bold preference for pants became a symbol of independence for women
in the 1930s, and in 1977 Diane Keaton made the menswear-look
famous again in *Annie Hall*.

The designs on the following pages celebrate the versatility of
menswear—as intended for men and as adapted for women and even
children. A military jacket joins a feminine silhouette with bold,
masculine details. Knitted ties, once reserved for the "suburban" man,
become unisex here. Knitter-friendly argyle patterns add a masculine
note to a vest and socks. And a Breton sailor's sweater—the classic striped,
boatneck design adopted by the French navy—here befits a little girl.

TOMBOYS

His-and-Her Llama Cardigan

I can't help thinking of this sweater as my "pépé" cardigan, after my grandfather, who still wears the same burgundy V-neck cardigan I remember from my childhood. I added a shawl collar and used a simple stitch pattern to showcase the shaping details at the neckline and shoulders.

Eager to demonstrate the cardigan's potential, I offer two here—one styled for men, but with snaps instead of buttons, and one for women, with short sleeves and hourglass shaping. As the bodies and sleeves are interchangeable, many variations are possible.

SIZES

X-Small (Small, Medium, Large, X-Large, 2X-Large, 3X-Large, 4X Large)
Long-sleeved cardigan shown
in size X-Large
Short-sleeved cardigan shown
in size Medium

FINISHED MEASUREMENTS

Chest: 34 (37½, 40¾, 44¼, 47½, 51, 54¼, 57¾)" (closed)

YARN

Classic Elite Montera (50% llama / 50% wool; 128 yds / 100 g):
13 (15, 17, 18, 18, 20, 21, 22) skeins in #3854 Alice blue heather for long-sleeved cardigan; 11 (12, 13, 15, 16, 17, 18, 19) skeins in #3827 cochineal for short-sleeved cardigan

NEEDLES

One 32" circular (circ) needle size US 7 (4.5 mm)
One pair straight needles size US 7 (4.5 mm)
Change needle size if necessary to obtain correct gauge.

NOTIONS

Stitch markers, stitch holders, yarn needle, sewing needle and matching thread, 5¾" leather shank buttons or ½" sew-on snaps

GAUGE

19 sts and 28 rows = 4" (10 cm) in Broken Rib

ABBREVIATIONS

Inc2: [K1, yo, k1] in next st
Wrp-t: Wrap next st, turn

STITCH PATTERNS

Twisted Rib (multiple of 2 sts + 1; 2-row rep)
Row 1 (RS): *K1-tbl, p1-tbl; rep from * to last st, k1-tbl.
Row 2: *P1-tbl, k1-tbl; rep from * to last st, p1-tbl.
Rep Rows 1 and 2 for Twisted Rib.

Broken Rib (multiple of 2 sts + 1; 2-row rep)
Row 1 (RS): Knit.
Row 2: *P1, k1; rep from * to last st, p1.
Rep Rows 1 and 2 for Broken Rib.

NOTES

▸ Work edge sts in St st, except for lower sleeve cuff. Cuffs on long sleeves are turned back; edge sts are worked in rev St st for first 18 rows so that seaming can be done from the WS.
▸ Shaping is done with double increases and decreases to maintain continuity of rib pattern.
▸ All shoulder shaping is worked on Back *only* using a combination of decreases and short rows; the shoulder seam falls to the back.

Long-Sleeved Cardigan

BACK

CO 83 (91, 99, 107, 115, 123, 131, 139) sts.

Twisted Rib Border: (RS) K1 (edge st), work Twisted Rib to last st, k1 (edge st). Maintaining edge sts in St st, work 11 more rows in Twisted Rib.

Begin Broken Rib: (RS) Maintaining edge sts in St st, work in Broken Rib until Back measures 15¾ (16¼, 16¾, 17½, 18, 18½, 19¼, 19¾)", ending with a WS row.

Shape Armholes: (RS) Maintaining patt as est, dec 2 sts at each edge on next row, then every other row 3 (4, 5, 6, 7, 8, 9, 10) more times as follows: K3, sssk, knit to last 6 sts, k3tog, k3—67 (71, 75, 79, 83, 87, 91, 95) sts rem. Work even in patt as est until armholes measure 5¾ (6, 6¼, 6½, 7¼, 7½, 7¾, 8)", ending with a WS row.

Shape Shoulders:
Row 1 (RS): K4, wrp-t.
Row 2: P1, k1, p2.

Row 3: K3, sssk, knit to last 6 sts, k3tog, k3.

Row 4: P2, k1, p1, wrp-t.

Row 5: K4.

Row 6: P2, k1, p3tog, work in patt to last 6 sts, sssp, k1, p2.

Rep [Rows 1–6] 5 (5, 6, 6, 6, 7, 7, 8) more times and [Rows 1–3] 0 (1, 0, 1, 1, 0, 1, 0) time(s)—19 (19, 19, 19, 23, 23, 23, 23) sts rem. Place sts on holder for Back neck.

LEFT FRONT

CO 38 (42, 46, 50, 54, 58, 62, 66) sts.

Twisted Rib Border: (RS) K1, *p1-tbl, k1-tbl; rep from * to last st, k1. Maintaining edge sts in St st, work 11 more rows in Twisted Rib as est.

Begin Broken Rib: (RS) Maintaining edge sts in St st and continuing rib as est from border, work even in Broken Rib until Front measures 15¾ (16¼, 16¾, 17½, 18, 18½, 19¼, 19¾)", ending with a WS row.

Shape Armhole: Set-up row (RS): Ssk, k2, sssk, knit to end—35 (39, 42, 47, 51, 55, 59, 63) sts rem. Work 1 WS row.

Dec 2 sts at armhole edge on next row, then every other row 2 (3, 4, 5, 6, 7, 8, 9) more times as follows: K3, sssk, knit to end—29 (31, 33, 35, 37, 39, 41, 43) sts rem. Work 1 WS row.

Shape Neck: (RS) Dec 2 sts at neck edge on next row, then every 24 (24, 24, 16, 16, 20, 20) rows 2 (2, 2, 2, 3,

3, 3, 3) more times as follows: Work in patt as est to last 6 sts, k3tog, k3—23 (25, 27, 29, 29, 31, 33, 35) sts rem. Work 6 (6, 10, 10, 12, 12, 4, 4) rows even in patt as est. BO all sts.

RIGHT FRONT

CO 38 (42, 46, 50, 54, 58, 62, 66) sts.

Twisted Rib Border: (RS) K1, *k1-tbl, p1-tbl; rep from * to last st, k1. Maintaining edge sts in St st, work 11 more rows in Twisted Rib as est.

Begin Broken Rib: (RS) Maintaining edge sts in St st and continuing rib as est from border, work even in Broken Rib until piece measures 15¾ (16¼, 16¾, 17½, 18, 18½, 19¼, 19¾)", ending with a WS row.

Shape Armhole: Set-up row (RS): Work in patt as est to last 7 sts, k3tog, k2, k2tog—35 (39, 42, 47, 51, 55, 59, 63) sts rem. Work 1 WS row. Dec 2 sts at armhole edge on next row, then every other row 2 (3, 4, 5, 6, 7, 8, 9) more times as follows: Work in patt as est to last 6 sts, k3tog, k3—29 (31, 33, 35, 37, 39, 41, 43) sts rem. Work 1 WS row.

Shape Neck: (RS) Dec 2 sts at neck edge on next row, then every 24 (24, 24, 16, 16, 20, 20) rows 2 (2, 2, 2, 3, 3, 3) more times as follows: K3, sssk, knit to end—23 (25, 27, 29, 29, 31, 33, 35) sts rem. Work 6 (6, 10, 10, 12, 12, 4, 4) rows even. BO all sts.

LONG SLEEVES (make 2)

CO 44 (44, 46, 46, 48, 48, 50, 54) sts.

Twisted Rib Cuffs: (RS) P1, *k1-tbl, p1-tbl; rep from * to last st, p1. Maintaining edge sts in rev St st (see Notes), work even in Twisted Rib as est for 17 more rows. Beg working edge sts in St st and work 6 more rows in Twisted Rib.

Shape Sleeves: (RS) Maintaining edge sts in St st and continuing rib as est from cuff, begin Broken Rib. Inc 2 sts each edge on 3rd row, then every

16 rows 7 (0, 0, 0, 0, 0, 0, 0) times,
every 14 rows 0 (8, 4, 0, 0, 1, 0, 0)
times, every 12 rows 0 (0, 5, 6, 1, 4, 0,
0) times, every 10 rows 0 (0, 0, 4, 10, 0,
3, 8) times, and every 8 rows 0 (0, 0, 0,
0, 7, 10, 5) times as follows: K4, Inc2,
knit to last 4 sts, Inc2, k3, working all
new sts in patt—76 (80, 86, 90, 96, 100,
106, 110) sts. Work even until sleeve
measures 22¾ (22¾, 22½, 22½, 22¼,
22¼, 22, 22)" from beg, ending with a
WS row.

Shape Cap: Set-up row (RS): Ssk, k2,
sssk, knit to last 6 sts, k3tog, k3.
Work 1 WS row in patt as est. Dec 2 sts
each edge on next row, then every
other row 2 (3, 4, 5, 6, 7, 8, 9) more
times as follows: K3, sssk, knit to last
6 sts, k3tog, k3—59 (59, 61, 61, 63, 63,
65, 65) sts rem. BO all sts.
Go to Finishing section to complete
Cardigan.

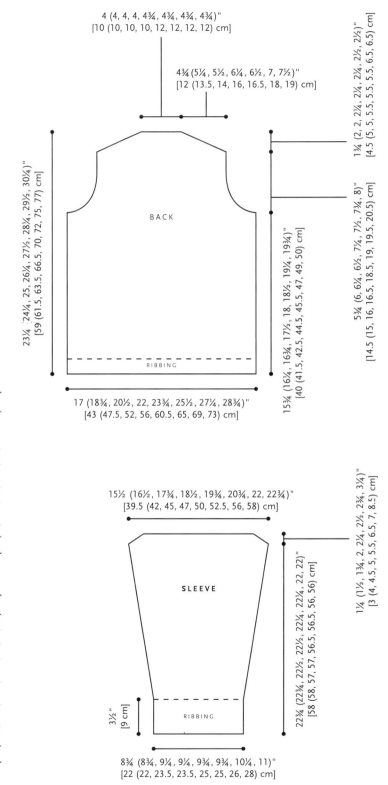

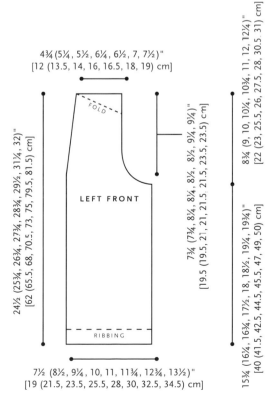

Short-Sleeved Cardigan

BACK

CO 83 (91, 99, 107, 115, 123, 131, 139) sts.

Twisted Rib Border: (RS) K1 (edge st), work Twisted Rib to last st, k1 (edge st). Maintaining edge sts in St st, work 11 more rows in Twisted Rib.

Begin Broken Rib: (RS) Maintaining edge sts in St st, work in Broken Rib for 8 rows.

Shape Waist: (RS) Set-up row: K4, pm, k17 (21, 25, 29, 33, 37, 41, 45), pm, k41, pm, k17 (21, 25, 29, 33, 37, 41, 45), pm, k4. Work 1 WS row.

Decrease for Waist: (RS) Dec 8 sts on next row as follows: Knit to marker, sm, k3tog, knit to next marker, sm, sssk, knit to 3 sts before next marker, k3tog, sm, knit to 3 sts before last marker, sssk, sm, k3. Work 17 (19, 21, 23, 25, 27, 29, 31) rows even in patt as est. Work Dec row. Work 11 rows even. Work Dec row—59 (67, 75, 83, 91, 99, 107, 115) sts rem. Work 5 rows even.

Increase for Upper Body: (RS) Inc 8 sts on next row as follows: Knit to marker, sm, Inc2, knit to marker, sm, Inc2, knit to 1 st before next marker, Inc2, sm, knit to 1 st before last marker, Inc2, sm, k3. Work 11 rows even in patt as est. Work Inc row. Work 17 (19, 21, 23, 25, 27, 29, 31) rows even. Work Inc row—83 (91, 99, 107, 115, 123, 131, 139) sts. Work even in patt as est until piece measures 15¾ (16¼, 16¾, 17½, 18, 18½, 19¼, 19¾)", ending with a WS row.

Shape Armholes: (RS) Dec 2 sts each edge on next row, then every other row 3 (4, 5, 6, 7, 8, 9, 10) more times as follows: K3, sssk, knit in patt as est to last 6 sts, k3tog, k3—67 (71, 75, 79, 83, 87, 91, 95) sts rem. Work even until armholes measure 5¾ (6, 6¼, 6½, 7¼, 7½, 7¾, 8)", ending with a WS row.

Shape Shoulders:

Row 1 (RS): K4, wrp-t.

Row 2: P1, k1, p2.

Row 3: K3, sssk, knit to last 6 sts, k3tog, k3.

Row 4: P2, k1, p1, wrp-t.

Row 5: K4.

Row 6: P2, k1, p3tog, work in patt to last 6 sts, sssp, k1, p2.

Rep [Rows 1–6] 5 (5, 6, 6, 6, 7, 7, 8) more times and [Rows 1–3] 0 (1, 0, 1, 1, 0, 1, 0) time(s)—19 (19, 19, 19, 23, 23, 23, 23) sts rem. Place sts on holder for Back neck.

LEFT FRONT

CO 38 (42, 46, 50, 54, 58, 62, 66) sts.

Twisted Rib Border: (RS) K1, *p1-tbl, k1-tbl; rep from * to last st, k1. Maintaining edge sts in St st, work 11 more rows in Twisted Rib as est.

Begin Broken Rib: (RS) Maintaining edge sts as in St st and continuing rib as est from border, work 8 rows in Broken Rib.

Shape Waist: Set-up row (RS): K4, pm, k17 (21, 25, 29, 33, 37, 41, 45), pm, knit to end. Work 1 WS row.

Decrease for Waist: (RS) Dec 4 sts on next row as follows: Knit to marker, sm, k3tog, knit to next marker, sm, sssk, knit to end. Work 17 (19, 21, 23, 25, 27, 29, 31) rows even in patt as est. Work Dec row. Work 11 rows even. Work Dec row— 26 (30, 34, 38, 42, 46, 50, 54) sts rem. Work 5 rows even.

Increase for Upper Body: (RS) Inc 4 sts on next row as follows: Knit to marker, sm, Inc2, knit to marker, sm, Inc2, knit to end. Work 11 rows even in patt as est. Work Inc row. Work 17 (19, 21, 23, 25, 27, 29, 31) rows even. Work Inc row—38 (42, 46, 50, 54, 58, 62, 66) sts. Work even in patt as est until piece measures 15¾ (16¼, 16¾, 17½, 18, 18½, 19¼, 19¾)", ending with a WS row.

RIGHT FRONT

CO 38 (42, 46, 50, 54, 58, 62, 66) sts.

Twisted Rib Border: (RS) K1, *k1-tbl, p1-tbl; rep from * to last st, k1. Maintaining edge sts in St st, work 11 more rows in Twisted Rib as est.

Begin Broken Rib: (RS) Maintaining edge sts in St st and continuing rib as est from border, work 8 rows in Broken Rib.

Shape Waist: Set-up row (RS): K17, pm, knit to last 4 sts, pm, k4. Work 1 WS row.

Decrease for Waist: (RS) Dec 4 sts on next row as follows: *Knit to 3 sts before marker, k3tog, sm, knit to 3 sts before next marker, sssk, sm, k4. Work 17 (19, 21, 23, 25, 27, 29, 31) rows even in patt as est. Work Dec row. Work 11 rows even. Work Dec row—26 (30, 34, 38, 42, 46, 50, 54) sts rem. Work 5 rows even.

Increase for Upper Body: (RS) Inc 4 sts on next row as follows: *Knit to 1 st before marker, Inc2, sm; rep from * to last 4 sts, k4. Work 11 rows even in patt as est. Work Inc row. Work 17 (19, 21, 23, 25, 27, 29, 31) rows even. Work Inc row—38 (42, 46, 50, 54, 58, 62, 66) sts. Work even in patt as est until piece measures 15¾ (16¼, 16¾, 17½, 18, 18½, 19¼, 19¾)", ending with a WS row.

Shape Armhole: (RS) Set-up row: Work in patt as est to last 7 sts, k3tog, k2,

Shape Armhole: Set-up row (RS): Ssk, k2, k3tog, knit to end. Work 1 WS row. Dec 2 sts at armhole edge on next row, then every other row 2 (3, 4, 5, 6, 7, 8, 9) more times as follows: K3, sssk, knit to end—29 (31, 33, 35, 37, 39, 41, 43) sts rem. Work 1 WS row.

Shape Neck: (RS) Dec 2 sts at neck edge on next row, then every 24 (24, 24, 24, 16, 16, 20, 20) rows 2 (2, 2, 2, 3, 3, 3, 3) more times as follows: Knit to last 6 sts, k3tog, k3—29 (31, 33, 35, 37, 39, 41, 43) sts rem. Work 6 (6, 10, 10, 12, 12, 4, 4) rows even. BO all sts.

k2tog—35 (39, 42, 47, 51, 55, 59, 63) sts rem. Work 1 WS row. Dec 2 sts at armhole edge on next row, then every other row 2 (3, 4, 5, 6, 7, 8, 9) more times as follows: Work in patt as est to last 6 sts, k3tog, k3—29 (31, 33, 35, 37, 39, 41, 43) sts rem. Work 1 WS row.
Shape Neck: (RS) Dec 2 sts at neck edge on next row, then every 24 (24, 24, 24, 16, 16, 20, 20) rows 2 (2, 2, 2, 3, 3, 3, 3) more times as follows: K3, sssk, knit to end—23 (25, 27, 29, 29, 31, 33, 35) sts rem. Work 6 (6, 10, 10, 12, 12, 4, 4) rows even. BO all sts.

SHORT SLEEVES (make 2)
CO 68 (72, 78, 82, 88, 92, 98, 102) sts.
Twisted Rib Border: (RS) K1, *k1-tbl,

p1-tbl; rep from * to last st, end k1. Maintaining edge sts in St st, work 9 more rows in Twisted Rib as est.
Begin Broken Rib: (RS) Maintaining edge sts in St st and continuing rib as est from border, work 14 (12, 12, 10, 10, 10, 8, 8) rows in Broken Rib, ending with a WS row.
Shape Sleeves: (RS) Inc 2 sts each edge on next row, then on following 6th row as follows: K4, Inc2, knit to last 4 sts, Inc2, k3—76 (80, 86, 90, 96, 100, 106, 110) sts. Work even until Sleeve measures 5 (5, 5, 5, 5½, 5½, 5½, 5½)", ending with a WS row.
Shape Cap: (RS) Set-up row: Ssk, k2, sssk, knit to last 6 sts, k3tog, k3. Work 1 WS row in patt as est. Dec 2 sts each

edge on next row, then every other row 2 (3, 4, 5, 6, 7, 8, 9) more times as follows: K3, sssk, knit to last 6 sts, k3tog, k3—59 (59, 61, 61, 63, 63, 65, 65) sts rem. BO all sts.

FINISHING
(All Cardigans)
Sew shoulder seams.
Collar: (RS) Beg at lower border, pick up and knit 113 (117, 123, 129, 133, 137, 143, 147) sts along right Front; work Twisted Rib across 19 (19, 19, 19, 23, 23, 23, 23) Back neck sts; pickup and knit 113 (117, 123, 129, 133, 137, 143, 147) sts along left Front—245 (253, 265, 277, 289, 297, 309, 317) sts.
Rows 1 and 3 (WS): Slip 1 wyif, *k1-tbl, p1-tbl; rep from * across.
Row 2: Slip 1 wyib, *p1-tbl, k1-tbl; rep from * across.
Row 4 (Buttonhole row-Men's [optional]): Maintaining patt as est, work to last 70 (70, 72, 72, 74, 74, 76, 76) sts, k2tog-tbl, [yo] twice, *work 14 (14, 14, 14, 16, 16, 16, 16) sts, k2tog-tbl, [yo] twice; rep from * 3 more times, work to end.
Row 4 (Buttonhole row-Women's [optional]): Maintaining patt as est, work 4 (4, 6, 6, 4, 4, 6, 6) sts, k2tog-tbl, [yo] twice, *work 14 (14, 14, 14, 16, 16, 16, 16) sts, k2tog-tbl, [yo] twice; rep from * 3 more times, work to end.
Shape Collar:
Row 5: Maintaining patt as est, slipping all yo's as you come to them and dropping 2nd yo, work 80 (80, 82, 82, 84, 84, 86, 86) sts, pm, work 33 (37, 41, 47, 49, 53, 57, 61) sts, Inc2, pm, work 17 (17, 17, 17, 21, 21, 21, 21) sts, pm, Inc2, work 33 (37, 41, 47, 49, 53, 57, 61) sts, pm, work 80 (80, 82, 82, 84, 84, 86, 86) sts.
Row 6: Work to last marker, turn.
Note: A gap will form at turn.
Row 7: Yo, work to first marker, turn.
Rows 8–20, *excluding Rows 9, 13, 17, and 21:* Yo, work to 4 (4, 4, 4, 6, 6, 6, 6) sts before gap, turn.

Rows 9, 13, 17, and 21: Yo, work to 1 st before first Back neck marker, Inc2, work to next marker, sm, Inc2, work to 4 (4, 4, 4, 6, 6, 6, 6) sts before gap, turn. 265 (273, 285, 297, 309, 317, 329, 334) sts rem.
Row 22: Yo, work in patt, closing all gaps by working yo's and next st as p2tog-tbl.
Row 23: Work in patt as est, closing gaps on opposite band by working yo's and next st as ssk.
Work 1 row even, then BO all sts loosely.

Block pieces to measurements. Mark shoulder fold on fronts. *(Note: This will be below the actual seam, which falls to the back.)* Sew in sleeves, centering top of cap at marked fold. Sew side and sleeve seams. Sew on snaps *or* buttons. Weave in loose ends.

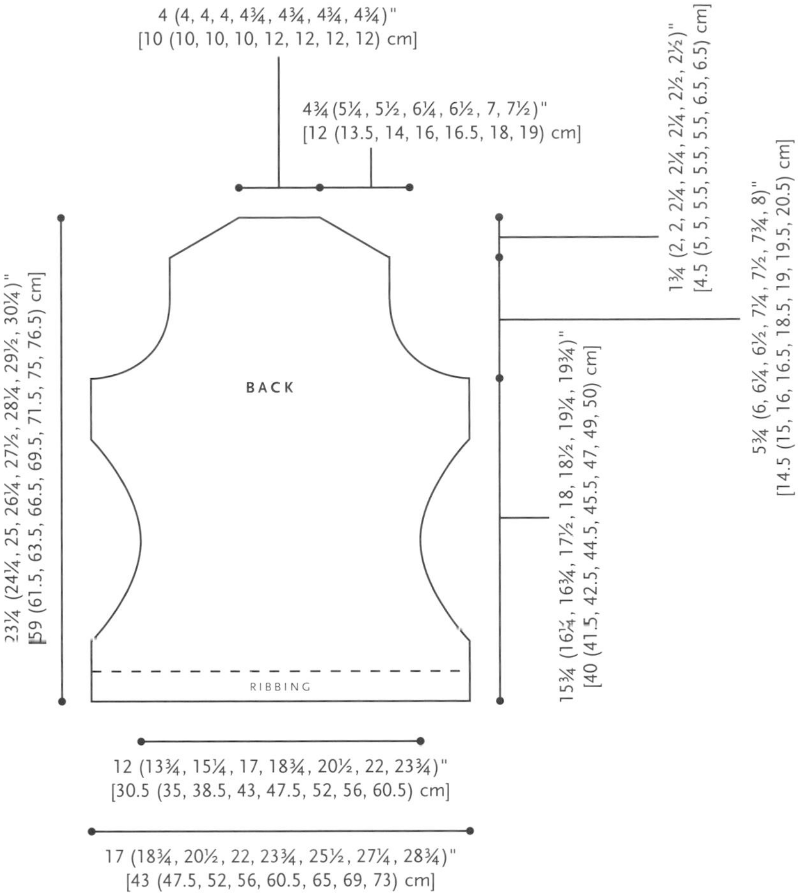
4 (4, 4, 4, 4¾, 4¾, 4¾, 4¾)"
[10 (10, 10, 10, 12, 12, 12, 12) cm]
4¾ (5¼, 5½, 6¼, 6½, 7, 7½)"
[12 (13.5, 14, 16, 16.5, 18, 19) cm]
1¾ (2, 2, 2¼, 2¼, 2¼, 2½, 2½)"
[4.5 (5, 5, 5.5, 5.5, 5.5, 6.5, 6.5) cm]
5¾ (6, 6¼, 6½, 7¼, 7½, 7¾, 8)"
[14.5 (15, 16, 16.5, 18.5, 19, 19.5, 20.5) cm]
23¼ (24¼, 25, 26¼, 27½, 28¼, 29½, 30¼)"
[59 (61.5, 63.5, 66.5, 69.5, 71.5, 75, 76.5) cm]
BACK
15¾ (16¼, 16¾, 17½, 18, 18½, 19¼, 19¾)"
[40 (41.5, 42.5, 44.5, 45.5, 47, 49, 50) cm]
RIBBING
12 (13¾, 15¼, 17, 18¾, 20½, 22, 23¾)"
[30.5 (35, 38.5, 43, 47.5, 52, 56, 60.5) cm]
17 (18¾, 20½, 22, 23¾, 25½, 27¼, 28¾)"
[43 (47.5, 52, 56, 60.5, 65, 69, 73) cm]

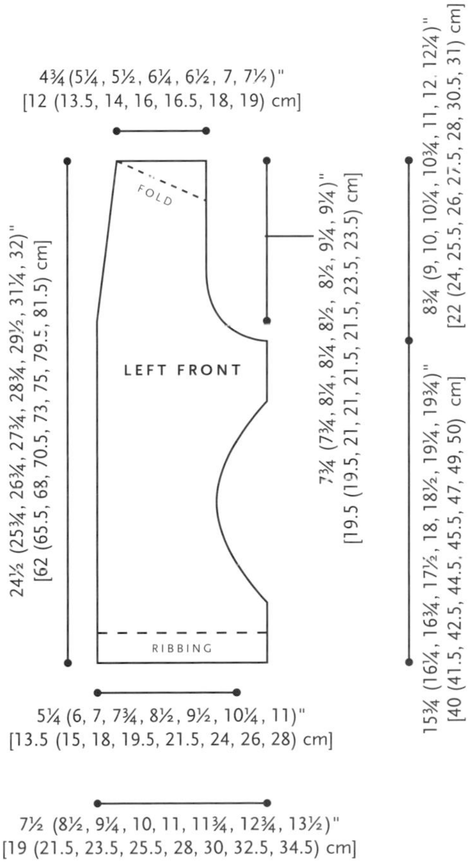
4¾ (5¼, 5½, 6¼, 6½, 7, 7½)"
[12 (13.5, 14, 16, 16.5, 18, 19) cm]
FOLD
LEFT FRONT
RIBBING
24½ (25¾, 26¾, 27¾, 28¾, 29½, 31¼, 32)"
[62 (65.5, 68, 70.5, 73, 75, 79.5, 81.5) cm]
7¾ (7¾, 8¼, 8¼, 8½, 8½, 9¼, 9¼)"
[19.5 (19.5, 21, 21, 21.5, 21.5, 23.5, 23.5) cm]
8¾ (9, 10, 10¼, 10¾, 11, 12, 12¼)"
[22 (24, 25.5, 26, 27.5, 28, 30.5, 31) cm]
15¾ (16¼, 16¾, 17½, 18, 18½, 19¼, 19¾)"
[40 (41.5, 42.5, 44.5, 45.5, 47, 49, 50) cm]
5¼ (6, 7, 7¾, 8½, 9½, 10¼, 11)"
[13.5 (15, 18, 19.5, 21.5, 24, 26, 28) cm]
7½ (8½, 9¼, 10, 11, 11¾, 12¾, 13½)"
[19 (21.5, 23.5, 25.5, 28, 30, 32.5, 34.5) cm]

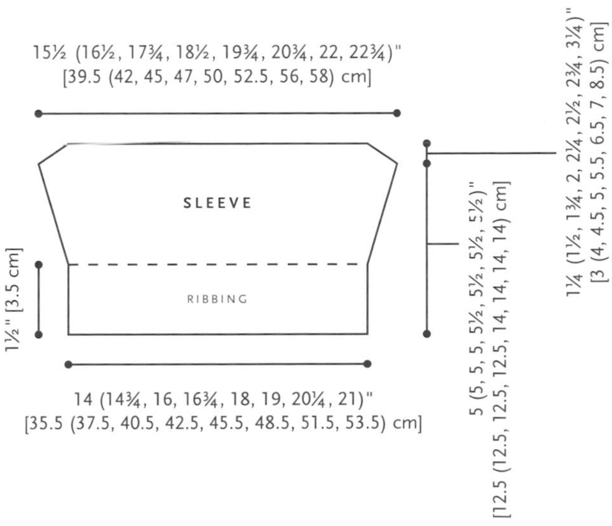
15½ (16½, 17¾, 18½, 19¾, 20¾, 22, 22¾)"
[39.5 (42, 45, 47, 50, 52.5, 56, 58) cm]
SLEEVE
RIBBING
1½" [3.5 cm]
5 (5, 5, 5½, 5½, 5½, 5½, 5½)"
[12.5 (12.5, 12.5, 14, 14, 14, 14, 14) cm]
1¼ (1½, 1¾, 2, 2¼, 2½, 2¾, 3¼)"
[3 (4, 4.5, 5, 5.5, 6.5, 7, 8.5) cm]
14 (14¾, 16, 16¾, 18, 19, 20¼, 21)"
[35.5 (37.5, 40.5, 42.5, 45.5, 48.5, 51.5, 53.5) cm]

Aspen Top-Down Sweater

SIZES
X-Small (Small, Medium, Large,
X-Large, 2X-Large)
Shown in size Medium

FINISHED MEASUREMENTS
Chest: 33¼ (37, 39½, 43, 45½, 48)"

YARN
GGH Aspen (50% merino wool / 50%
microfiber; 62 yds / 50 g): 9 (10, 10, 13,
13, 15) balls #5 dark red

NEEDLES
One each 16" and 32" circular (circ)
needles size US 9 (5.5 mm)
One each 16" and 32" circular needles
size US 10½ (6.5 mm)
One set of five double-pointed needles
(dpn) size US 9 (5.5 mm)
One set of five double-pointed needles
size US 10½ (6.5 mm)
Change needle size if necessary to
obtain correct gauge.

NOTIONS
Stitch markers (one in contrasting
color for beg of rnd), coiless safety pin,
yarn needle, cable needle (cn)

GAUGE
13 sts and 24 rnds = 4" (10 cm) in
Twisted Rib Pattern using larger needle

ABBREVIATION
Inc2: (K1, yo, k1) in next st

STITCH PATTERN
Twisted Rib
(multiple of 2 sts; 1-rnd rep)
Rnd 1: [K1-tbl, p1-tbl] around.
Rep Rnd 1 for Twisted Rib.

The fisherman's sweater is a traditional garment frequently featuring textural stitchwork that is knit in many European coastal communities, often by fishermen's wives for their husbands or for export, to be practical, warm, and weatherproof. Among the better known are the English, Scottish, and Portuguese versions.

My version is inspired by English fishermen's sweaters knit primarily in brioche stitch from the top down. I've incorporated twisted-stitch panels into it for added depth and interest. This sweater is easily custom-fitted by adding stitches on either side of the center cable panel until the desired circumference is reached, and then knitting until it is long enough for the intended wearer.

YOKE

Neck Rib: Using smaller 16" circ needle, CO 72 (88, 88, 104, 104, 120) sts. Place marker (pm) for beg of rnd and join, being careful not to twist sts. Work 3 rnds of Twisted Rib.

NOTES
- This garment is worked in-the-round from the top down. The yoke is worked first, the sleeve sts are put on hold while the body is worked, and the sleeves are worked last.
- All slipped stitches are worked with yarn in back.
- Change to longer circ needle on Body when necessary to accommodate sts.
- In order to maintain stitch pattern on Sleeves, 2 sts are decreased at center underarm as follows: Work to 1 st before marked center st, then if center st is knit, p3tog; if center st is purled, k3tog-tbl.

Change to larger 16" circ needle.
Next rnd: [Slip 1, p1] around.
Shape Yoke:
Rnd 1 (set-up and inc): *K1-tbl, pm; p1, Inc2, [p1, k1-tbl] 0 (1, 1, 2, 2, 3) time(s), p1, work Rnd 1 of Chart A over center 5 sts, p1, [k1-tbl, p1] 0 (1, 1, 2, 2, 3) time(s), Inc2, p1, pm; k1-tbl, pm; p1, Inc2, [p1, k1-tbl] 0 (1, 1, 2, 2, 3) time(s), p1, work Rnd 1 of Chart B over center 17 sts, p1, [k1-tbl, p1] 0 (1, 1, 2, 2, 3) time(s), Inc2, p1, pm; rep from * to end of rnd, omitting last marker—16 sts inc'd; 88 (104, 104, 120, 120, 136) sts.
Rnd 2: *Slip 1, sm, p1, k1-tbl, p1, k1-tbl, purl the purl sts and slip the knit sts across to 4 sts before next marker, k1-tbl, p1, k1-tbl, p1, sm; rep from * 3 more times.
Rnds 3 and 5: Cont in patt as est, working increased sts in rib, knitting all knit sts tbl, and working charts over center sts as est.
Rnds 4 and 6: Cont in patt as est, slipping all knit sts and purling all purl

sts on rib, and working Charts over center sts as est.

Rep [Rnds 1–6] 5 (5, 6, 6, 7, 7) times, working increased sts in rib and 8-rnd reps of panel sts over center sts as est—168 (184, 200, 216, 232, 248) sts. Work even in patts as est until yoke measures approx 7¼ (7½, 8, 8¼, 8½, 9)" from beg.

Divide for Body and Sleeves: Removing markers, place first 35 (39, 43, 47, 51, 55) sts on holder for Sleeve; CO 3 (3, 3, 4, 4, 4) sts for underarm, pm for beg of rnd; CO 4 (4, 4, 5, 5, 5) sts for underarm; work 49 (53, 57, 61, 65, 69) sts in patt as est; place next 35 (39, 43, 47, 51, 55) sts on second holder for Sleeve; CO 7 (7, 7, 9, 9, 9) sts for underarm; work in patt as est to end of rnd—112 (120, 128, 140, 148, 156) sts on needle.

BODY

Work even in patt as est until Body measures approx 5¾ (6¾, 7½, 8½, 9, 10½)", or 1¾" short of desired finished length, ending with Rnd 14 of panel repeat. Work last 8 rnds of Chart B for rib set-up.

Bottom Rib: Change to smaller needle, and work 3 rnds of Twisted Rib, then BO loosely in rib.

SLEEVES (make 2)

With larger dpns, work 35 (39, 43, 47, 51, 55) sts from holder in patt as est, pick up and knit 7 (7, 7, 9, 9, 9) sts from underarm—42 (46, 50, 56, 60, 64) sts. Mark center underarm st with coiless safety pin for beg of rnd, moving it up as work progresses. Working underarm sts in rib as est, work 2 rnds even.

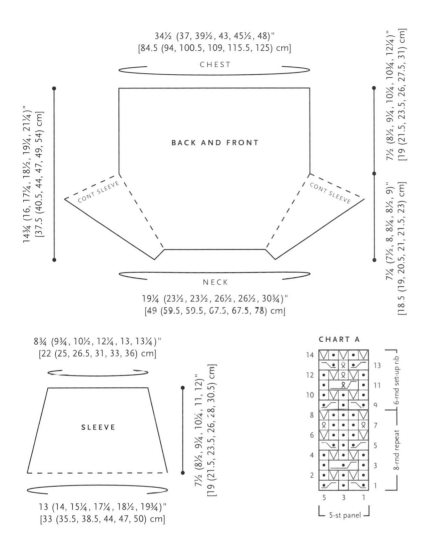

34½ (37, 39½, 43, 45½, 48)"
[84.5 (94, 100.5, 109, 115.5, 125) cm]

CHEST

BACK AND FRONT

14¾ (16, 17¼, 18½, 19¼, 21¼)" [37.5 (40.5, 44, 47, 49, 54) cm]

CONT SLEEVE

CONT SLEEVE

7½ (8½, 9¼, 10¼, 10¾, 12¼)" [19 (21.5, 23.5, 26, 27.5, 31) cm]

7¼ (7½, 8, 8¼, 8½, 9)" [18.5 (19, 20.5, 21, 21.5, 23) cm]

NECK

19¼ (23½, 23½, 26½, 26½, 30¾)"
[49 (59.5, 59.5, 67.5, 67.5, 78) cm]

8¾ (9¾, 10½, 12¼, 13, 13¼)"
[22 (25, 26.5, 31, 33, 36) cm]

SLEEVE

7½ (8½, 9¼, 10¼, 11, 12)" [19 (21.5, 23.5, 26, 28, 30.5) cm]

13 (14, 15¼, 17¼, 18½, 19¾)"
[33 (35.5, 38.5, 44, 47, 50) cm]

KEY

⊗ K1-tbl

• Purl

∨ Slip 1 st purlwise wyib.

Slip next st to cn, hold to front, p1, k1-tbl from cn.

Slip next st to cn, hold to back, k1-tbl, p1 from cn.

Slip 2 sts to cn, hold to back, k1-tbl, slip second st from cn back to left-hand needle, p1, k1-tbl from cn.

Slip 2 sts to cn, hold to back, k1-tbl, slip second st from cn back to left-hand needle, k1-tbl, k1-tbl from cn.

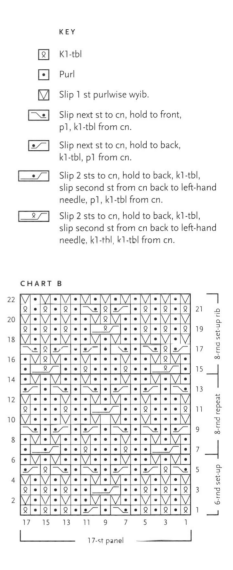

CHART A

6-rnd set-up rib
8-rnd repeat
5-st panel

CHART B

8-rnd set-up rib
8-rnd repeat
6-rnd set-up
17-st panel

Shape Sleeves: Dec 2 sts at center underarm on next rnd, then every 6 rnds 6 (6, 7, 7, 8, 8) more times as follows: Work in patt to 1 st before marked center st, p3tog or k3tog-tbl (see Notes), cont around—28 (32, 34, 40, 42, 46) sts rem. AT THE SAME TIME, when Sleeve measures approx 4½ (5½, 6¼, 7¼, 8, 9)", or 3" short of desired finished

length, finish 8-rnd rep, then work last 6 rnds of Chart A for rib set-up. **Cuff Rib:** Change to smaller dpns, and work 8 rnds of Twisted Rib. BO loosely in rib.

FINISHING
Weave in all ends. Block to finished measurements.

Rustic Elegant Tie

FINISHED MEASUREMENTS

Women's: 1¼" wide by 53" long
(shown in red)
Men's: 1¾" wide by 56" long
(shown in purple)

YARN

La Lana Plant Dyed Bombyx Silk
(100% silk; 59 yds / 1 oz): 2 skeins
rajah red
or
La Lana Phat Silk Fines (50% Bombyx
silk / 50% fine wool; 71 yds / 1 oz):
2 skeins purple

NEEDLES

Two double-pointed needles (dpn)
size US 3 (3.25 mm)
Change needle size if necessary to
obtain correct gauge.

NOTIONS

Coiless safety pin or yarn marker,
yarn needle

GAUGE

30 sts and 36 rows = 4" (10 cm) in
Moss Stitch

STITCH PATTERN

Moss Stitch
(odd number of sts; 4-row rep)
Row 1 (RS): Slip 1 wyib, [k1, p1]
across.
Row 2: Slip 1 wyif, [p1, k1] across.
Row 3: Slip 1 wyib, [p1, k1] across.
Row 4: Slip 1 wyif, [k1, p1] across.
Rep Rows 1–4 for Moss Stitch.

Hanging on my dining room wall is a 1953 framed *Esquire* print I found in an old Montreal menswear store. On it are illustrations of six men dressed for different occasions: Formal Evening, Semi-formal Evening, V.I.P. in Town, Business, Suburban, and Sportswear. While *Esquire* categorized knit ties as suburban, the reality is much broader. Today this British mainstay is favored by a wide variety of men and women from Ivy Leaguers to rebels, who, depending on their mood, wear them casually with jeans or a miniskirt, or more formally with a tweed suit. Made from a small amount of gorgeous, naturally dyed silk, this tie provides a wonderful accent to any wardrobe.

Using tubular CO method (see Special Techniques, page 136), CO 8 (12) sts.
First 2 rows: [Slip 1 wyib, k1] across.
Establish Moss Stitch: Work Row 1 of Moss st, increasing 1 st—9 (13) sts. Work even in Moss st as established until tie measures approx 20 (14)", ending with Row 4 of patt.
Decrease Row: Slip 1 wyib, p2tog, work in patt as est to last 3 sts, ssp, k1—7 (11) sts.

[Men's tie only]: Work even in patt as est until piece measures 20", then rep Dec row—7 (9) sts.
[Both ties]: Work even in patt as est until piece measures 24". Place a marker in fabric to indicate beg of back neck section.

BACK NECK SECTION

Row 1: [K1, slip 1 wyif] to last st, k1.
Rows 2 and 4: Purl.
Row 3: K1 [Slip 1 wyif, k1] across.
Rep last 4 rows until back neck section measures approx 13 (14)" from marker.

Change back to Moss st and work even until tie measures 53 (56)" or desired length, dec 1 st on last row— 8 (12) sts rem.
Next 2 rows: [Slip 1 wyib, k1] across. BO all sts using tubular BO method (see Special Techniques, page 136).

CHILD'S NAUTICAL PULLOVER

SIZES
Children's 2 (4, 6, 8)
Shown in size 6

FINISHED MEASUREMENTS
Chest: 24 (28, 32, 36)"

YARN
Jo Sharp Soho Summer DK (100%
cotton; 110 yd / 50 g): 4 (5, 6, 8) balls
#219 sailboat (MC); 2 (2, 2, 3) balls
#227 putty (CC)

NEEDLES
One pair straight needles size US 3
(3.25 mm)
One pair straight needles size US 2
(3 mm)
Change needle size if necessary to
obtain correct gauge.

NOTIONS
Yarn needle, stitch markers

GAUGE
24 sts and 30 rows = 4" (10 cm) in
Scalloped Stripe using larger needles

STITCH PATTERN
Scalloped Stripe
(multiple of 12 sts; 6-row rep)
Row 1 (RS): With MC, *[k2tog] twice,
[yo, k1] 3 times, yo, [ssk] twice, k1; rep
from *.
Row 2: Purl, working all yarnovers
through back loops.
Rows 3 and 4: With CC, work in St st.
Rows 5 and 6: With MC, work in St st.
Rep Rows 1–6 for Scalloped Stripe.

While it is difficult to say precisely when the tradition began, stripes have been part of sailors' uniforms since at least the mid-17th century. Of these uniforms, my favorite is the sailor shirt (or *marinière*, in French), a long-sleeved, striped tee from Brittany traditionally knit in navy and off-white, and favored by personalities as varied as Gabrielle Chanel, Marcel Marceau, and Pablo Picasso.

I originally knit a women's marinière similar to this one in a finer yarn for *Interweave Knits* magazine. I redid it here for young girls with the same playfully undulating stripes, but in colors closer to those of the traditional sailor shirt. The nautical look is a perennial favorite for children, and they can get in and out of the wide boat neck with ease.

BACK
Using smaller needles, MC, and the long tail method, CO 74 (86, 98, 110) sts. **Establish Rib:** (WS) K2, *p2, k2; rep from * across. Work even in Rib for 10 rows. Change to larger needles and St st. Work even until piece measures 2½ (2¾, 3, 3½)", ending with a WS row. **Establish Scalloped Stripe:** (RS) K1 (edge st), work Scalloped Stripe patt over center 72 (84, 96, 108) sts, k1 (edge st). Maintaining edge sts in St st, work even in Scalloped Stripe until Back measures 8 (9¾, 11½, 13)" from beg, ending with a WS row. **Shape Armholes:** (RS) BO 3 (4, 5, 5) sts at beg of next 2 rows—68 (78, 88, 100) sts. Dec 1 st at each edge on next row, then every other row 2 (2, 3, 5) times, then every 4 rows 0 (2, 3, 4) times as follows: K2, k2tog, work in patt to last 4 sts, ssk, k2—62 (68, 74, 80) sts rem. AT THE SAME TIME, after working Rows 1–6 of Scalloped Stripe 8 (10, 13, 15) times total, work Rows 1 and 2 once more, then change to St st. Work even until armholes

measure 4 (4¾, 5½, 6½)", ending with a RS row. **Begin Back Neck Rib:** (WS) P2 (3, 2, 2), k2, *p2, k2; rep from * to last 2 (3, 2, 2) sts, p2 (3, 2, 2). Work 7 rows in Rib as est. Using the sewn method (see Special Techniques, page 136), BO all sts.

FRONT
Work as for Back until armholes measure 1¾ (2½, 2¾, 3¾)", ending with a WS row. **Shape Left Neck (short rows):** (RS) K19 (22, 24, 25), turn; yo, place marker (pm), purl to end. *Next row (RS):** Knit to 2 sts before marker, turn; yo, pm, purl to end. Rep from * 6 (6, 8, 8) more times— 5 (8, 6, 7) sts rem. **Next row (RS):** Knit all sts, removing markers and hiding gaps by knitting each yo together with the following st. **Shape Right Neck (short rows):** (WS) P19 (22, 24, 25), turn; yo, pm, knit to end. *Next row (WS):** Purl to 2 sts before marker, turn; yo, pm, knit to end.

Rep from * 6 (6, 8, 8) more times—5 (8, 6, 7) sts rem.

Next row (WS): Purl all sts, removing markers and hiding gaps by working ssp with each yo and the following st. Knit 1 row.

Begin Front Neck Rib: (WS) P2 (3, 2, 3), k2, *p2, k2; rep from * to last 2 (3, 2, 3) sts, p2 (3, 2, 3). Work 7 rows in Rib as est. Using the sewn method, BO all sts.

SLEEVE

Using smaller needles, MC, and the long tail method, CO 42 (46, 50, 50) sts.

Establish Rib: (RS) K2, *p2, k2; rep from *. Work even in Rib as est for 9 more rows.

Shape Sleeve: (RS) Change to larger needles and beg St st. Inc 1 st at each edge on this row, then every 16 rows 2 (3, 3, 0) times, every 14 rows 0 (0, 2, 0) times, and every 10 rows 0 (0, 0, 9) times as follows: K2, M1-L, knit to last 2 sts, M1-R, k2—48 (54, 62, 70) sts. Work even until Sleeve measures 8 (10½, 13¾, 16)" from beg, ending with a WS row.

Shape Cap: (RS) BO 3 (4, 5, 5) sts at beg of next 2 rows. Dec 1 st at each edge on next row, then every 4 rows 0 (1, 1, 1) time(s), then every other row 10 (9, 10, 13) times as follows: K2, ssk, knit to last 4 sts, k2tog, k2—20 (24, 28, 32) sts rem. BO 3 (4, 4, 4) sts at beg of next 2 rows—14 (16, 20, 24) sts rem. BO all sts.

FINISHING

Weave in loose ends. Block pieces to measurements. Using yarn needle, baste back shoulders over front shoulders, overlapping them by about 2½". Sew in sleeves, sewing through both front and back fabric at shoulders. Sew side and sleeve seams, being careful to match stripes at sides. Steam lightly.

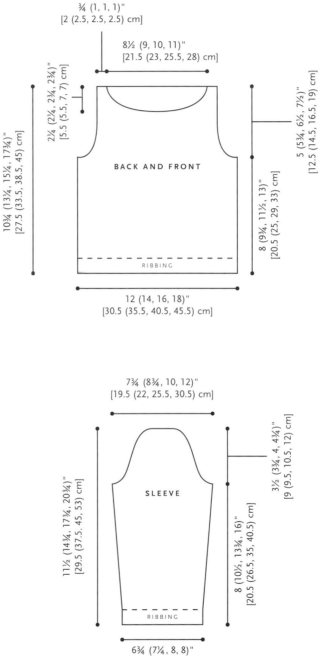

¾ (1, 1, 1)"
[2 (2.5, 2.5, 2.5) cm]

8½ (9, 10, 11)"
[21.5 (23, 25.5, 28) cm]

2¼ (2¼, 2¾, 2¾)"
[5.5 (5.5, 7, 7) cm]

5 (5¾, 6½, 7½)"
[12.5 (14.5, 16.5, 19) cm]

10¾ (13¾, 15¼, 17¾)"
[27.5 (33.5, 38.5, 45) cm]

BACK AND FRONT

8 (9¾, 11½, 13)"
[20.5 (25, 29, 33) cm]

RIBBING

12 (14, 16, 18)"
[30.5 (35.5, 40.5, 45.5) cm]

7¾ (8¾, 10, 12)"
[19.5 (22, 25.5, 30.5) cm]

3½ (3¾, 4, 4¾)"
[9 (9.5, 10.5, 12) cm]

11½ (14¾, 17¾, 20¾)"
[29.5 (37.5, 45, 53) cm]

SLEEVE

8 (10½, 13¾, 16)"
[20.5 (26.5, 35, 40.5) cm]

RIBBING

6¾ (7¼, 8, 8)"
[17 (18.5, 20.5, 20.5) cm]

ARGYLE SOCKS

SIZE
To fit men's US shoe size 9–11

FINISHED MEASUREMENTS
Foot circumference: 9"
Leg length: 9"

YARN
Louet Gems Opal (100% wool; 225 yds / 100 g): 2 skeins caribou (MC); 1 skein each fern green (A) and linen grey (B)

NEEDLES
One set of five double-pointed needles (dpn) size US 2 (2.75 mm) Change needle size if necessary to obtain correct gauge.

NOTIONS
Stitch marker, yarn needle

GAUGE
26 sts and 40 rows = 4" (10 cm) in Stockinette stitch (St st)

ABBREVIATIONS
N1, N2, N3, N4: Needles 1, 2, 3, 4 (N1 and N4 are sole, N2 and N3 are instep)

NOTE
▸ The sock is worked using MC only. After the sock is finished, the diagonal color pattern is created by working Duplicate Stitch (see Special Techniques, page 136), using A and B, following Chart.

Even during the heyday of argyle hand-knitting in the 1930s, many patterns weren't graphed, and knitters were forced to follow line-by-line instructions. So it comes as no surprise that many chose to avoid allover argyle patterning and contented themselves with knitting socks with several horizontal bands instead. The simplified version is also faster and easier to complete, an advantage to busy knitters then as today.

My ambitious first attempt at these socks, inspired by a photograph of Louis Armstrong wearing argyles and golf knickers, was in full intarsia. Though pretty in effect, the numerous color changes compromised the elasticity of the sock leg, which I had trouble getting over my foot. I decided on a more knitter-friendly approach: a monochromatic sock whose argyle pattern is embroidered on afterward.

LEG
CO 60 sts. Distribute evenly on four needles; place marker (pm) for beg of rnd and join, being careful not to twist sts. Work K2, P1 Rib for 1". Beg Chart, working Rnds 1-30 twice, then Rnds 1–16 once more—leg measures approx 8½".

HEEL FLAP
Slip sts from second needle to first needle. Working back and forth on these sts only, knit heel flap as follows:
Row 1 (RS): *Slip 1 wyib, k1; rep from * to end.
Row 2: Slip 1, purl to end.
Rep these 2 rows 14 more times.

TURN HEEL
Row 1 (RS): Slip 1, k15, ssk, k1, turn.
Row 2: Slip 1, p3, p2tog, p1, turn.
Row 3: Slip 1, k4, ssk, k1, turn.
Cont working in this manner, working 1 additional st before the decrease on each row, until 18 sts rem, ending with a WS row.

Next row: Slip 1, k14, ssk, turn.
Next row: Slip 1, p14, p2tog, turn—16 sts rem.

SHAPE GUSSET
Pick-up rnd: N1: Slip 1, k15 across heel flap, then pick up 15 sts along the side of the heel, then pick up a st from the row below the first instep st to prevent a hole; N2 and N3: k15 on each needle; N4: pick up a st from the row below the first heel st to prevent a hole, then pick up 15 sts along the side of the heel; N1: knit the first 8 sts. Pm for beg of rnd—78 sts arranged 24–15–15–24.
Rnd 1: N1: Knit to last 3 sts, k2tog, k1; N2 and N3: knit; N4: k1, ssk, knit to end.
Rnd 2: Knit around.
Rep [Rnds 1 and 2] 8 more times—60 sts rem (15 sts each needle).

FOOT
Work even until foot measures 9" from heel, or 2" short of desired finished length.

ARGYLE CHART

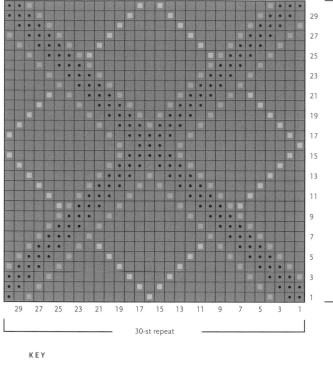

29
27
25
23
21
19
17
15
13
11
9
7
5
3
1

30-rnd repeat

29 27 25 23 21 19 17 15 13 11 9 7 5 3 1

30-st repeat

KEY

- ⬜ MC - Knit
- ⬛ MC - Purl
- ⬜ MC - Knit; A - duplicate st
- ⬜ MC - Knit; B - duplicate st

SHAPE TOE

Rnd 1: *N1: Knit to last 3 sts, k2tog, k1;
N2: k1, ssk, knit to end; rep from *
across N3 and N4—56 sts rem.
Rnd 2: Knit around.
Rep [Rnds 1 and 2] 6 more times—32
sts rem.
Rep [Rnd 1] 5 times—12 sts rem.
Break yarn, leaving an 8" tail.
Slip sts from N4 to N1 and from N2 to
N3. Holding N1 and N3 parallel, graft
sts using Kitchener st (see Special
Techniques, page 136).

FINISHING

Work diagonal lines using Duplicate
Stitch (see Special Techniques, page
136), following Chart. Weave in ends
on inside of sock.

ARGYLE VEST

SIZES
Men's X-Small (Small, Medium, Large, X-Large, 2X-Large)
Shown in size Large

FINISHED MEASUREMENTS
Chest: 34¼ (38, 42, 45¾, 49½, 53¼)"

YARN
Louet Sales Gems Topaz (100% wool; 168 yds / 100 g): 4 (4, 5, 5, 6, 6) skeins #53 caribou (MC); 1 skein each #49 charcoal (A) and #43 pewter (B)

NEEDLES
One pair straight needles size US 5 (3.75 mm)
One pair straight needles size US 6 (4 mm)
One each 16" and 24" circular (circ) needles size US 5 (3.75 mm)
Change needle size if necessary to obtain correct gauge.

NOTIONS
Stitch markers, bobbins (optional for Intarsia), yarn needle

GAUGE
21 sts and 28 rows = 4" (10 cm) in Stockinette stitch (St st) using larger needles

Argyle patterns, thought to have originated from the attempt to knit plaids, are an integral part of British style and have been a standby for well over a hundred years. Never completely out of fashion, they have often been used in an exaggerated manner by British designers such as Bill Gibb, Vivienne Westwood, and Paul Smith. Their send-ups defy convention, as argyle patterns exemplify upper-class tradition for so many of us that simply scaling them up or coloring them in unexpected or jarring hues can signify rebellion. I didn't aim for rebellion with this piece, but simply doodled arrangements of lozenges until I hit upon a pleasing combination.

BACK

Hem: Using smaller needles, MC, and long-tail method, CO 92 (102, 112, 122, 132, 142) sts. Beg with a WS row, work 6 rows in St st. Knit 1 WS row (turning row). Change to larger needles and work even in St st until Back measures 13¼ (13½, 13¾, 14, 14¼, 14½)", ending with a WS row.

Shape Armholes: (RS) BO 5 (6, 7, 8, 9, 10) sts at beg of next 2 rows—82 (90, 98, 106, 114, 122) sts rem. Dec 1 st at armhole edges on next row, every other row 2 (5, 6, 10, 11, 13) more times, then every 4 rows 3 (2, 2, 0, 0, 0) times as follows: K2, ssk, knit to last 4 sts, k2tog, k2—70 (74, 80, 84, 90, 94) sts rem. Work even until armholes measure 10 (10, 10¼, 10½, 10½, 10¾)", ending with a WS row.

Shape Back Neck and Shoulders: (RS) Mark center 22 (24, 26, 28, 28, 30) sts for Back Neck placement. Knit to first marker, join a second ball of yarn and BO center 22 (24, 26, 28, 28, 30) sts, knit to end—24 (25, 27, 28, 31, 32) sts each side. Working each side at the same time, dec 1 st at each neck edge

every RS row 4 (5, 5, 5, 6, 6) times as follows: Knit to last 4 sts, ssk, k2; k2 k2tog, knit to end. AT THE SAME TIME, at each armhole edge, BO 3 sts 2 (2, 4, 3, 5, 4) times, then BO 4 sts 2 (2, 1, 2, 1, 2) time(s)—6 sts rem at each side. BO all rem sts.

FRONT

Hem: Using smaller needles, MC, and long-tail method, CO 92 (102, 112, 122, 132, 142) sts. Beg with a WS row, work 6 rows in St st. Knit 1 WS row (turning row). Change to larger needles.

Establish Intarsia Pattern: (RS) K13 (16, 18, 21, 23, 26), place marker (pm), work Row 1 of 27-st panel (see Chart), pm, k12 (16, 22, 26, 32, 36), pm, work 27-st panel, pm, knit to end. Slipping markers on every row, work even in patt as est until Front measures 13¼ (13½, 13¾, 14, 14¼, 14½)", ending with a WS row.

Shape Armholes and V-neck: (RS) Shape armholes as for Back. AT THE SAME TIME, when Front measures 16¾ (16¼, 16¼, 16½, 16¼, 16½)", pm between center sts. Working both sides at the same time and joining a second

ball of yarn on first row at center, shape V-neck as follows:

Rows 1 and 3 (RS): Knit to 4 sts before center, ssk, k2; k2, k2tog, knit to end.
Rows 2, 4, 5, and 6: Work even in patt as est.

Rep [Rows 1–6] 6 (7, 8, 8, 9, 9) more times, then work [Rows 1 and 2] 1 (1, 0, 1, 0, 1) time(s)—20 (20, 22, 23, 25, 26) sts rem each side.

Work even until armholes measure same as for Back to shoulders, ending with a WS row.

Shape Shoulders: (RS) At each armhole edge, BO 3 sts 2 (2, 4, 3, 5, 4) times, then BO 4 sts 2 (2, 1, 2, 1, 2) time(s)—6 sts rem each side. BO all rem sts.

FINISHING

Using a yarn needle, sew shoulder seams. Sew side seams. Turn up hem facing along turning row, and sew to WS.

Armbands: (RS) Using shorter circ needle and MC, beg at side seam, pick up and knit 108 (108, 112, 112, 116, 116) sts evenly spaced around armhole. Pm for beg of rnd and join. Purl 1 rnd. Work K2, P2 Rib for ¾". BO in rib.
Neckband: (RS) Using longer circ needle and MC, beg at right shoulder seam, pick up and knit 36 (40, 42, 44, 46, 48) sts across Back neck, 46 (46, 47, 48, 49, 50) sts along left Front neck, pm, 46 (46, 47, 48, 49, 50) sts along right Front neck—128 (132, 136, 140, 144, 148) sts total. Pm for beg of rnd and join. Purl 1 rnd.
Establish K2, P2 Rib: P1 (1, 0, 0, 2, 1), k2 (2, 2, 1, 2, 2), [p2, k2] to 3 sts before

Front neck marker, p2, k1, sm, k1, p2,
cont in K2, P2 Rib to end of rnd.
Dec 1 st on either side of Front neck
marker on next rnd, then every other
rnd 3 more times as follows: Work
in rib as est to 2 sts before marker,
k2tog, sm, ssk, work in rib as est to
end of rnd—120 (124, 128, 132, 136,
140) sts. BO in rib.

Weave in loose ends. Block to finished
measurements.

KEY

Note: Work in St st.

- ■ MC
- ▢ A
- ■ B

ARGYLE CHART

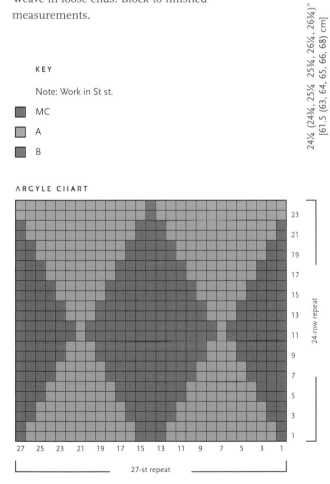

27-st repeat

24-row repeat

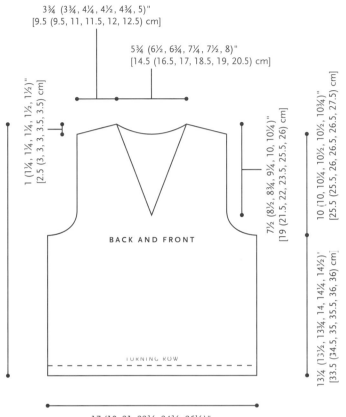

3¾ (3¾, 4¼, 4½, 4¾, 5)"
[9.5 (9.5, 11, 11.5, 12, 12.5) cm]

5¾ (6½, 6¾, 7¼, 7½, 8)"
[14.5 (16.5, 17, 18.5, 19, 20.5) cm]

1 (1¼, 1¼, 1¼, 1½, 1½)"
[2.5 (3, 3, 3, 3.5, 3.5) cm]

7½ (8½, 8¾, 9¼, 10, 10¼)"
[19 (21.5, 22, 23.5, 25.5, 26) cm]

10 (10, 10¼, 10½, 10½, 10¾)"
[25.5 (25.5, 26, 26.5, 26.5, 27.5) cm]

24¼ (24¾, 25¼, 25¾, 26¼, 26¾)"
[61.5 (63, 64, 65, 66, 68) cm]

13¼ (13½, 13¾, 14, 14¼, 14½)"
[33.5 (34.5, 35, 35.5, 36, 36) cm]

BACK AND FRONT

TURNING ROW

17 (19, 21, 22¾, 24¾, 26½)"
[43 (48.5, 53.5, 58, 63, 67.5) cm]

Mohair Portrait Scarf

FINISHED MEASUREMENTS
Approximately 10" wide by 52" long

YARN
Needful Yarns Mohair Royal (80% mohair / 20% nylon; 235 yds / 25 g): 2 balls #1650 off-white

NEEDLES
One set of five double-pointed needles (dpn) size US 6 (4 mm) Change needle size if necessary to obtain correct gauge.

NOTIONS
Yarn needle

GAUGE
22 sts and 28 rows = 4" (10 cm) in Right Diagonal Lace pattern after blocking; exact gauge is not essential.

NOTE
▸ To work the Diagonal Lace patterns correctly, you must change the position of the beg of rnd between patterns as follows:
Move marker left: Remove marker, K1, replace marker.
Move marker right: Remove marker and slip last st to LH needle; replace marker and slip st back to RH needle.

Ruffs, starched neckpieces made of lace or fabric gathered into deep, regular folds, were worn by European men and women in the 16th and 17th centuries. The most extreme examples, known as cartwheel ruffs, stuck out more than a foot and required a metal framework to support them. Many countries passed sumptuary laws to limit or forbid their use, and ruffs eventually fell out of favor, although they are still worn by English choir boys and those who hold certain positions in British law. Gwyneth Paltrow wore one in the 1998 movie *Shakespeare in Love*, as did Judi Dench playing Queen Elizabeth I. In fact, Queen Elizabeth's portrait in a bone ruff by Nicholas Hilliard is one of the most famous paintings of the English Renaissance.

This very different take on the ruff, knit in a soft kid mohair, is as nice to play with as it is to wear. Because of the versatile tube design, it can also be worn as a stole, neck gaiter, or scarf. The increases and decreases within it create pleats when the scarf is collapsed vertically, and gentle undulations when it is laid flat.

CO 120 sts. Place marker (pm) for beg of rnd and join, being careful not to twist sts.

*RIGHT DIAGONAL LACE
Rnd 1: Knit.
Rnd 2: [Yo, k2tog] around.
Work [Rnds 1–2] 8 times total.
Dec rnd: Move marker left. [K3tog, k1] around—60 sts.

LEFT DIAGONAL LACE
Rnd 1: [Ssk, yo] around.
Rnd 2: Knit.
Work [Rnds 1–2] 7 times, then rep Rnd 1 once more.
Inc rnd: [(K1, yo, k1) in next st, k1] around—120 sts. Move marker right.

RIGHT DIAGONAL LACE
Set-up rnd: [Yo, k2tog, yo, ssk] around.
Work [Rnds 1–2] of Right Diagonal Lace patt 8 times.

Repeat from * 5 more times.

Loosely BO all sts.

FINISHING
Weave in ends. Wet-block to open up lace patt.

MILITARY JACKET

SIZES
Small (Medium, Large, X-Large)
Shown in size Small

FINISHED MEASUREMENTS
Chest: 37½ (41¾, 46¼, 50¾)"

YARN
Cascade Eco Wool (100% wool;
478 yds / 250 g): 3 (4, 4, 4) skeins
#0515 navy

NEEDLES
One 32" circular (circ) needle size
US 8 (5 mm)
One double-pointed needle (dpn) size
US 8 (5 mm) or smaller
Change needle size if necessary to
obtain correct gauge.

NOTIONS
Stitch markers, stitch holders,
yarn needle, cable needle (cn), twelve
⅞" buttons, and ten ⅝" buttons

GAUGES
23 sts and 24 rows = 4" (10 cm) in
Cable pattern (Chart A or C)
18 sts and 24 rows = 4" (10 cm) in
Stockinette stitch (St st)

ABBREVIATIONS
Dec1-back: Slip 2 sts to cn and hold in
back, k1, k2tog from cn.
Dec1-front: Slip 1 st to cn and hold in
front, k1, slip st on cn back to LH
needle and ssp with next st.
Inc1-back: Slip 1 st to cn and hold in
back, k1, yo, k1 from cn.
Inc1-front: Slip 1 st to cn and hold in
front, k1, yo, k1 from cn.
C3B (Cable 3 Back): Slip 2 sts to cn and
hold in back, k1, k2 from cn.
C3F (Cable 3 Front): Slip 1 st to cn and
hold in front, k2, k1 from cn.

As I pondered what to include in this book, I turned for inspiration to reproductions of vintage texts such as Weldon's *Practical Needlework* magazine from the late 1800s and Butterick's 1892 *Art of Knitting*. Though some of the patterns illustrated in their pages are foreign to modern sensibilities, others are every bit as captivating as the ones found in contemporary magazines.

The little jackets I discovered in these books—with very simple shapes and basic cable arrangements—inspired this cardigan, which still looks current today. With "uniform chic" in mind, I added masculine touches such as back vents and buttoned cuffs, as well as a dramatic double-breasted front panel incorporating a collar. Although bold, the cables are satisfyingly simple; to complement them, I chose the biggest, boldest shank buttons I could find.

LEFT BACK VENT
Peplum: CO 25 (27, 29, 31) sts. Knit
3 rows.

One-row buttonhole: Slip 1 st to RH
needle and bring yarn to front of work
between needles; [slip to LH needle and
pass 2nd st on RH needle over it] 3 times.
Pass yarn over RH needle from front to
back and pass first st on RH needle over
it. Using the backward loop method (see
Special Techniques, page136), CO 4 sts.
Slip last CO st to LH needle and k2tog-tbl.

NOTES
▸ Sleeves and Back are worked in
  multiple pieces (2 and 3, respectively)
  to form vents, and are then joined into
  single pieces.
▸ Work all edge sts in St st.
▸ Slip all markers as you come to them.

Row 1 (RS): K4, [work Row 1 of Chart A,
pm, p4 (5, 6, 7)] twice, end k1 (edge st).
Row 2: P1 (edge st), work sts as they
appear to last 4 sts, k4.
Maintaining edge st and 4-st Garter
edging, work even until piece measures
2¼", ending with a WS row.
Shape Waist: (RS) Dec 2 sts on next row,
then every 4 rows twice more as follows:
[Work in patt to marker, sm, p2tog]
twice, work in patt to end—19 (21, 23,
25) sts rem. Work 3 rows, removing
markers. Break yarn and set aside,
leaving sts on needle.

CENTER BACK PANEL
Peplum: CO 98 (104, 110, 116) sts.
Knit 3 rows.
Row 1 (RS): K4, work Row 1 of Chart B,
[p4 (5, 6, 7), pm, work Row 1 of Chart
A] 3 times, pm, p6, pm, [work Row 1 of
Chart C, p4 (5, 6, 7), pm] 3 times, work
Row 1 of Chart B, end k4.
Row 2: K4, work sts as they appear to

last 4 sts, k4. Maintaining 4-st Garter edgings, work even until piece measures 2¼", ending with a WS row.

Shape Waist:

Dec row 1 (RS): Maintaining patt as est, [work to 2 sts before marker, p2tog] 3 times; work to next (4th) marker, [p1, p2tog] twice, sm; [work to 2 sts before marker, p2tog] 3 times; work in patt to end—90 (96, 102, 108) sts rem. Work 3 rows even.

Dec row 2 (RS): Maintaining patt as est, [work to 2 sts before marker, p2tog] 3 times; work to next (4th) marker, [p2tog] twice, sm; [work to 2 sts before marker, p2tog] 3 times; work in patt to end—82 (88, 94, 100) sts rem. Work 3 rows even.

Dec row 3 (RS): Maintaining patt as est, [work to 2 sts before marker, p2tog] 3 times; knit to next (4th) marker, p2tog; [work to 2 sts before marker, p2tog] 3 times; work in patt to end—75 (81, 87, 93) sts rem. Work 3 rows even, removing all markers. Break yarn and set aside, leaving sts on needle.

RIGHT BACK VENT

Peplum: CO 25 (27, 29, 31) sts. Knit 3 rows.

Row 1 (RS): K1 (edge st), [p4 (5, 6, 7), pm, work Row 1 of Chart C] twice, end k4.

Row 2: K4, work sts as they appear to last st, p1 (edge st).

Maintaining edge st and 4-st Garter edging, work even until piece measures 2¼", ending with a WS row.

Shape Waist: (RS) Dec 2 sts on next row, then every 4 rows twice more as follows: K1, [purl to 2 sts before marker, p2tog, sm, work Chart C] twice, end k4—19 (21, 23, 25) sts rem. Work 3 rows even, removing markers. Do not break yarn.

UPPER BACK

Join Pieces: (RS) Using yarn attached to Right Back, [work to marker, rm] twice, work to last 4 sts, pm, place next 4 sts on dpn and hold parallel to and behind Center Back panel; [k2tog] 4 times (sts from Right Back and Center Back); [work to marker, rm] 7 times, work to last 4 sts, pm, then put last 4 sts on dpn, parallel to and in front of Left Back panel; [k2tog] 4 times (sts from Center Back and Left Back), work in patt to end, removing rem markers—105 (115, 125, 135) sts.

Continue to Shape Waist: (WS) *Cont in patt as est, work to 4 sts before marker, [k2tog] twice; rep from * once more, work to end. Work 1 row even—101 (111, 121, 131) sts.

Next row (RS): *Work to marker, k2tog; rep from * once more, work to end—99 (109, 119, 129) sts. Work even until Back measures 7½ (7¾, 8¼, 8½)", ending with a WS row.

Shape Upper Body: (RS) K1, p1; [Chart A, p1, M1, p0 (1, 2, 3)] twice; Chart B; [p0 (1, 2, 3), M1, p1, Chart C] 3 times; p1; [Chart A, p1, M1, p0 (1, 2, 3)] 3 times; Chart B; [p0 (1, 2, 3), M1, p1, Chart C] twice, p1, k1—109 (119, 129, 139) sts. Work even until Back measures 13¼ (13½, 13¾, 14)", ending with a WS row.

Shape Armholes: (RS) BO 4 (5, 6, 7) sts at beg of next 2 rows, and 3 (4, 5, 6) sts at beg of following 2 rows—95 (101, 107, 113) sts rem. Dec 1 st each edge every RS row 8 times as follows: K1, p1, p2tog, work in patt as est to last 4 sts, ssp, p1, k1—79 (85, 91, 97) sts rem.

Next row: (RS) K1, p2, Chart B; [p2tog] 0 (1, 2, 2) time(s); p2 (1, 0, 1), Chart A; [p2tog] 0 (1, 1, 2) time(s); p2 (1, 2, 1), Chart A; [p2tog] 0 (0, 1, 2) time(s); p2 (3, 2, 1), Chart A, p1, Chart C; [p2tog] 0 (0, 1, 2) time(s); p2 (3, 2, 1), Chart C; [p2tog] 0 (1, 1, 2) time(s); p2 (1, 2, 1), Chart C; [p2tog] 0 (1, 2, 2) time(s); p2 (1, 0, 1), Chart B, p2, k1—79 (81, 83, 85) sts rem.

[Continue for All Sizes]: Work even until armholes measure 7 (7½, 8, 8½)". Place rem sts on holder.

RIGHT FRONT

Peplum: CO 52 (57, 62, 67) sts. Knit 3 rows.

Next row (RS): K1 (edge st), p4 (5, 6, 7), pm, work Row 1 of Chart C, p4 (5, 6, 7), pm, work Row 1 of Chart B, [p4 (5, 6, 7), pm, work Row 1 of Chart A] twice, end p4 (5, 6, 7), k1 (edge st). Maintaining edge sts in St st, work even until piece measures 2¼".

Shape Waist: (RS) Dec 5 sts on next row, then every 4 rows twice more as follows: K1, purl to 2 sts before marker, p2tog; Chart C; purl to 2 sts before next marker, p2tog; Chart B; [purl to 2 sts before marker, p2tog, Chart A] twice; purl to last 3 sts, end p2tog, k1—37 (42, 47, 52) sts rem. Work even until Front measures 7½ (7¾, 8¼, 8½)", ending with a WS row.

Shape Upper Body: (RS) K1, p1, M1, p0 (1, 2, 3), Chart C; p1, M1, p0 (1, 2, 3); Chart B; [p0 (1, 2, 3), M1, p1, Chart A] twice; p1, M1, p0 (1, 2, 3), k1—42 (47, 52, 57) sts. Work even until Front measures 13¼ (13½, 13¾, 14)", ending with a RS row.

Shape Armhole: (WS) BO 4 (5, 6, 7) sts at beg of row, and 3 (4, 5, 6) sts at beg of following WS row—35 (38, 41, 44) sts rem. Dec 1 st at armhole edge on next 8 RS rows as follows: Work in patt to last 4 sts, ssp, p1, k1—27 (30, 33, 36) sts rem.

Next row:

Narrow Shoulders: (RS) K1; [p2tog] 0 (1, 1, 2) time(s); p2 (1, 2, 1), Chart C; [p2tog] 0 (1, 2, 2) time(s); p2 (1, 0, 1), Chart B, p3 (4, 5, 6), k1—27 (28, 30, 32) sts.

[Continue for All Sizes]: Work even until armhole measures 7 (7½, 8, 8½)". Place rem sts on holder.

LEFT FRONT

Peplum: CO 52 (57, 62, 67) sts. Knit 3 rows.

Next row (RS): K1 (edge st), [p4 (5, 6, 7), pm, work Row 1 of Chart C] twice, p4 (5, 6, 7), pm, work Row 1 of Chart B, p4 (5, 6, 7), pm, work Row 1 of Chart A, end p4 (5, 6, 7), k1 (edge st). Maintaining edge sts in St st, cont Charts and work other sts as they appear until piece measures 2¼".

Shape Waist: (RS) Dec 5 sts on next row, then every 4 rows twice more as follows: K1, purl to 2 sts before marker, p2tog; [Chart C, purl to 2 sts before marker, p2tog] twice; Chart B; purl to 2 sts before next marker, p2tog; Chart A; purl to last 3 sts, end p2tog, k1—37 (42, 47, 52) sts rem. Work even until Front measures 7½ (7¾, 8¼, 8½)", ending with a WS row.

Shape Upper Body: (RS) K1; [p1, M1, p0 (1, 2, 3), Chart C] twice; p1, M1, p0 (1, 2, 3); Chart B; p0 (1, 2, 3), M1, p1; Chart A; p1, M1, p0 (1, 2, 3), k1—42

(47, 52, 57) sts. Work even until Front measures 13¼ (13½, 13¾, 14)", ending with a WS row.

Shape Armholes: (RS) BO 4 (5, 6, 7) sts at beg of row, and 3 (4, 5, 6) sts at beg of following RS row—35 (38, 41, 44) sts rem. Dec 1 st at armhole edge every RS row 8 times as follows: K1, p1, p2tog, work in patt to end—27 (30, 33, 36) sts rem.

Next row:

Narrow shoulders: (RS) K1, p2, Chart B; [p2tog] 0 (1, 2, 2) time(s); p2 (1, 0, 1), Chart A, p2 (1, 2, 1); [p2tog] 0 (1, 1, 2) time(s); k1—27 (28, 30, 32) sts.

[Continue for All Sizes]: Work even until armhole measures 7 (7½, 8, 8½)". Place rem sts on holder.

RIGHT SLEEVE

Left Cuff Vent: CO 11 (12, 13, 14) sts. Knit 3 rows.

Next row (RS): K3 (4, 5, 6), work Row 1 of Chart C, p1, k1 (edge st). Working first 3 (4, 5, 6) sts in Garter st

and maintaining edge st in St st, work even until piece measures 3¾", ending with a WS row. Break yarn and set aside.

Right Cuff Vent: CO 43 (47, 51, 55) sts. Knit 3 rows.

Next row (RS): K1 (edge st), p1 [work Row 1 of Chart A, p2 (3, 4, 5)] twice; p2, work Row 1 of Chart C, p2 (3, 4, 5), work Row 1 of Chart C, k3 (4, 5, 6). Working last 3 (4, 5, 6) sts in Garter st and maintaining edge st in St st, work even until piece measures 3¾", ending with a WS row. Do not break yarn.

Join Vents: (RS) Using yarn attached to right vent, work 40 (43, 46, 49) right vent sts, pm; slip next 3 (4, 5, 6) sts to dpn and hold parallel to and in front of left vent; [k2tog] 3 (4, 5, 6) times (sts from left and right vents of cuff); work in patt to end—51 (55, 59, 63) sts rem. Work 1 WS row.

Next row: Work to marker, sm, p2tog, work in patt to end—50 (54, 58, 62) sts. Remove marker and work even until sleeve measures 4¼", ending with a WS row.

Shape Sleeve: (RS) Inc 1 st each edge on next row, then every 10 rows 7 (1, 0, 0) times, every 8 rows 0 (8, 8, 4) time(s), and every 6 rows 0 (0, 3, 9) times, working all new sts in rev St st, as follows: K1, p1, M1, work to last 2 sts, M1, p1, k1—66 (74, 82, 90) sts. Work even until Sleeve measures 17½ (18¼, 19, 19¾)", ending with a WS row.

Shape Cap: (RS) BO 4 (5, 6, 7) sts at beg of next 2 rows, and 3 (4, 5, 6) sts at beg of following 2 rows—52 (56, 60, 64) sts rem. Dec 1 st at each edge every

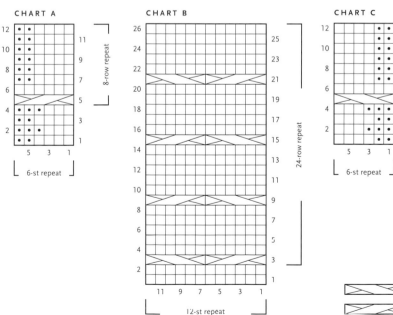

KEY

☐ Knit on RS, purl on WS.

⊡ Purl on RS, knit on WS.

⤬ Slip next 3 sts to cn, hold to front, k3, k3 from cn.

⤬ Slip next 3 sts to cn, hold to back, k3, k3 from cn.

RS row 17 (18, 19, 20) times as follows: K1, p1, p2tog, work to last 4 sts, end ssp, p1, k1—18 (20, 22, 24) sts rem. Work 1 WS row. BO all sts.

LEFT SLEEVE

Left Cuff Vent: CO 43 (47, 51, 55) sts. Knit 3 rows.

Next row (RS): K3 (4, 5, 6), work Row 1 of Chart A, p2 (3, 4, 5), work Row 1 of Chart A, p2 [work Row 1 of Chart C, p2 (3, 4, 5)] twice, work Row 1 of Chart C, end p1, k1 (edge st). Working first 3 (4, 5, 6) sts in Garter st and maintaining edge st in St st, work even until piece measures 3¾", ending with a WS row. Break yarn and set aside.

Right Cuff Vent: CO 11 (12, 13, 14) sts. Knit 3 rows.

Next row (RS): K1 (edge st), p1, work Row 1 of Chart A, k3 (4, 5, 6). Working last 3 (4, 5, 6) sts in Garter st and maintaining edge st in St st, work even until piece measures 3¾" (9.5 cm), ending with a WS row. Do not break yarn.

Join Vent: (RS) Using yarn attached to right vent, work 8 right cuff sts, pm; place next 3 (4, 5, 6) sts on dpn and hold parallel to and behind left vent; [k2tog] 3 (4, 5, 6) times (sts from left and right sides of cuff); work in patt to end—51 (55, 59, 63) sts rem. Work 1 WS row.

Next row: Work to marker, sm, p2tog, work in patt to end—50 (54, 58, 62) sts. Work even until Sleeve measures 4¼", ending with a WS row. Cont as for right Sleeve.

COLLAR AND FRONT PLACKETS

Join shoulders using the 3-needle BO method (see Special Techniques, page 136).

Pick-up row (RS): Beg on 4th row from bottom of Right Front, pick up and knit 92 (96, 100, 104) sts along Right Front, 25 sts along Back neck and

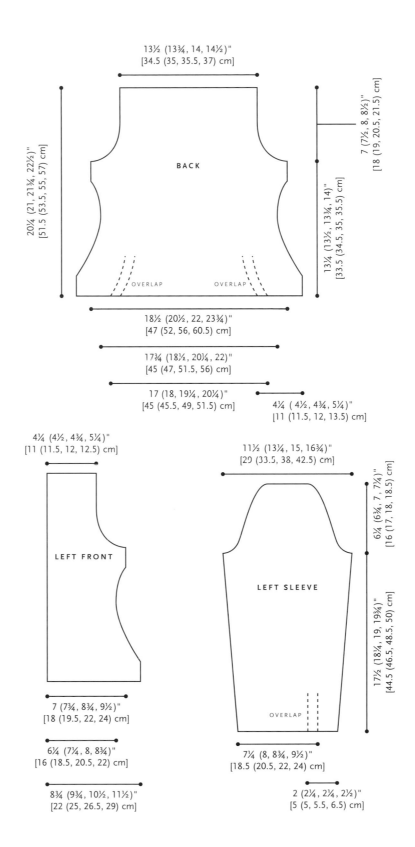

13½ (13¾, 14, 14½)"
[34.5 (35, 35.5, 37) cm]

BACK

7 (7½, 8, 8½)"
[18 (19, 20.5, 21.5) cm]

20¼ (21, 21¾, 22½)"
[51.5 (53.5, 55, 57) cm]

13¼ (13½, 13¾, 14)"
[33.5 (34.5, 35, 35.5) cm]

18½ (20½, 22, 23¾)"
[47 (52, 56, 60.5) cm]

OVERLAP   OVERLAP

17¾ (18¼, 20¼, 22)"
[45 (47, 51.5, 56) cm]

17 (18, 19¼, 20¼)"
[45 (45.5, 49, 51.5) cm]

4¼ (4½, 4¾, 5¼)"
[11 (11.5, 12, 13.5) cm]

4¼ (4½, 4¾, 5¼)"
[11 (11.5, 12, 12.5) cm]

11½ (13¼, 15, 16¾)"
[29 (33.5, 38, 42.5) cm]

6¼ (6¾, 7, 7¼)"
[16 (17, 18, 18.5) cm]

LEFT FRONT

LEFT SLEEVE

17½ (18¼, 19, 19¾)"
[44.5 (46.5, 48.5, 50) cm]

OVERLAP

7 (7¾, 8¾, 9½)"
[18 (19.5, 22, 24) cm]

6¼ (7¼, 8, 8¾)"
[16 (18.5, 20.5, 22) cm]

8¾ (9¾, 10½, 11½)"
[22 (25, 26.5, 29) cm]

7¼ (8, 8¾, 9½)"
[18.5 (20.5, 22, 24) cm]

2 (2¼, 2¼, 2½)"
[5 (5, 5.5, 6.5) cm]

92 (96, 100, 104) sts along Left Front, ending at same point of Left Front as for Right Front—209 (217, 225, 233) sts. Knit 1 WS row.

Set Up Pattern:

Row 1 (RS): K1 (edge st), p1, [Inc1-front, p2] 22 (23, 24, 25) times, pm, Inc1-front, pm, [p2, Inc1-front] 3 times, pm, k1, pm, [Inc1-back, p2] 3 times, pm, Inc1-back, pm, [p2, Inc1-back] 22 (23, 24, 25) times, p1, k1—261 (271, 281, 291) sts.

Row 2: P1, k1, [p3, Inc1-front] 22 (23, 24, 25) times, sm, p3, sm, [Inc1-front, p3] 3 times, sm, p1, [p3, Inc1-back] 3 times, sm, p3, sm, [Inc1-back, p3] 22 (23, 24, 25) times, end k1, p1—311 (323, 335, 347) sts.

Shape Collar Sides and Center Back Collar:

Row 3 (RS): K1, p1, [C3F, p3] to first marker, M1; sm, C3F, sm; M1, [p3, C3F] to next marker, sm; (k1, p1, k1) in same stitch, sm; [C3B, p3] to next marker, M1; sm, C3B, sm, M1, [p3, C3B] to last 2 sts, p1, k1—317 (329, 341, 353) sts.

Row 4: Work in est patt to first center back marker, sm; p1, pm, p1 (center st), pm, p1, sm; work in est patt to end of row.

Row 5: Work in patt as est to first marker, M1; sm, C3F, sm; M1, work in patt as est to next marker, sm; knit to first center-st marker, M1-R, sm, k1, sm, M1-L, knit to next marker, sm; work in patt as est to next marker, M1; sm, C3F, sm, M1, work in patt as est to last 2 sts, p1, k1—6 sts inc'd. Rep [Rows 4 and 5] 7 more times, then work Row 4 once more, continuing to work new side collar sts into patt as est and new center Back collar sts in St st—365 (377, 389, 401) sts.

Make Buttonholes and Shape Bottom Curve of Plackets:

Row 1 (RS): Maintaining patt as est, work 29 (35, 35, 41) sts, *make one-row buttonhole (see Notes), work 15 sts; rep from * 5 more times; cont in patt as est, increasing at markers as before, to last 6 sts; turn. *(Note: A gap will form at turn.)*

Row 2: Yo, work as est to last 6 sts, turn;

Row 3: Yo, work as est to 4 sts before gap, turn;

Row 4: Yo, work as est to 4 sts before gap, turn;

Rep Rows 3 and 4—383 (395, 407, 419) sts. Discontinue side and center collar increases and remove all markers except the 2 outlining center Back St st section. Rep Rows 3 and 4. Do not turn on last WS row; work to last yo and purl it together with following st; rep with all subsequent yo's.

Next row (RS): Work in patt as est around collar to yo and work it together with following st as ssp; rep with all subsequent yo's. Do not turn.

Establish Left Bottom Placket Border: With tip of RH needle, pick up and knit 16 sts along side of placket—399 (411, 423, 435) sts.

Decrease Cables: (WS) Dec 1 st as follows in each cable as it faces you: P21, *Dec1-front, p3; rep from * to marker, sm, purl center back collar sts, sm, *p3, Dec1-back; rep from * to last 2 sts, k1, p1—341 (351, 361, 371) sts. Do not turn.

Establish Right Bottom Placket Border: Using both needles to manipulate the yarn, pick up and purl 16 sts (so that edge st turns to the WS) along side of placket—357 (367, 377, 387) sts.

Decrease Cables: (RS) Dec 1 st in each cable as it faces you as follows: K18, *Dec1-front, p2; rep from * to 3 sts before marker, Dec1-front, sm, knit center Back sts, sm, Dec1-back, *p2, Dec1-back; rep from * to last 18 sts, knit to end—297 (305, 313, 321) sts.

Knit 3 rows. BO all sts.

FINISHING

Sew sleeves into armholes. Sew side and sleeve seams. Sew edges of lower placket edgings to fronts so that plackets and bottom front edges are aligned.

Sew 12 larger buttons to front (6 on each front placket), ¾" from pick-up line opposite buttonholes. Sew 5 smaller sleeve buttons on top of Garter edging, sewing though both layers.

Weave in loose ends. Block to finished measurements.

The 20th century was witness to the rise of a mass democratization—
brought about by an industrial revolution that began in the mid-1800s,
the rise of the middle class, and postwar booms—that afforded
new opportunities to more "ordinary" citizens than ever before.
Among these opportunities were increased global travel and, with it,
exposure to the ethnic influences and folk traditions of other cultures.
These global influences impacted and enriched many aspects of
Western culture, including fashion. Designers were quick to adapt
costume in both cut and ornamentation, and nary a decade has
gone by that fashion hasn't quoted another society in some way.
Knitters have been particularly fortunate, as talented authors such
as Lizbeth Upitis, Priscilla Gibson-Roberts, Richard Rutt, and so
many others have researched and presented invaluable information
on historical and folk knitting.

Relying on these researchers and others, I have borrowed
influences from knitting traditions worldwide—from Scandinavia to
South America, the Middle East, and the Far East—to create the
globally inspired pieces in this chapter. All are modern takes on
traditional fare: a soft Afghan sock with updated details, an *obi* that
goes beyond the kimono, fingerless mittens with Latvian patterning,
and a poncho fitted to suit modern silhouettes.

GLOBAL TRAVELERS

Beaded Pulse Warmers

FINISHED MEASUREMENTS
Circumference: 7"
Length: 4"

YARN
Grignasco Cashmere (100% cashmere; 240 yds / 25 g): 1 ball #564 navy

NEEDLES
One pair straight needles and one double-pointed needle (dpn) size US 0 (2 mm)
Change needle size if necessary to obtain correct gauge.

NOTIONS
Bead needle, waste yarn, yarn needle

BEADS
920 size 6 glass beads (extra beads are to allow for possible breakage and non-uniform beads)

GAUGE
24 sts and 46 rows = 4" (10 cm) in beaded Garter st pattern

ABBREVIATION
BUB (Bring up Bead): Slip 1 bead up next to stitch just worked

Many vintage and modern Norwegian publications feature designs for beaded cuffs. Also known as wrist or pulse warmers, they help to keep the body warm, alleviate joint pain, and, of course, beautify. Traditionally, they were worn by both men and women as part of Norwegian folk costume. The highly decorative beading technique used to create the pattern is actually quite simple: The knitter threads the appropriate number of beads onto the yarn before casting on, and then slips the beads into position between stitches according to the design.

PULSE WARMER (make 2)
Before Knitting: Using bead needle, string 440 beads onto yarn.
Using the provisional method (see Special Techniques, page 136), CO 24 sts. Knit 1 row.
Establish Pattern:
Row 1 (RS): K2, [BUB, k4] 5 times, BUB, k2.
Row 2 and all WS rows: Knit.
Row 3: K2, [BUB, k2] 11 times.

Row 5: K2, [BUB, k4] 5 times, BUB, k2.
Row 7: K2, [BUB, k1] 21 times, k1.
Row 8: Knit.
Rep [Rows 1–8] 9 more times.

FINISHING
Remove waste yarn from cast-on edge and transfer sts to dpn. With right sides held together, join edges using the 3-needle BO method (see Special Techniques, page 136). Weave in loose ends.

REGAL AFGHAN SLIPPERS

SIZES
Women's Small (Medium, Large)

FINISHED MEASUREMENTS
Foot circumference: 8½ (9½, 10¼)"

YARN
Reynolds Andean Alpaca Regal (90% alpaca / 10% wool; 110 yds / 100 g): 2 balls #2 silver grey (A), 1 ball #85 brown (B)

NEEDLES
One set of five double-pointed needles (dpn) size US 7 (4.5 mm) Change needle size if necessary to obtain correct gauge.

NOTIONS
Waste yarn, stitch marker, yarn needle, crochet hook

GAUGE
18 sts and 24 rnds = 4" (10 cm) in Stockinette stitch (St st)

ABBREVIATIONS
N1, N2, N3, N4: Needles 1, 2, 3, 4

STRIPE PATTERN
6 rnds B, 6 rnds A.

NOTE
▶ This sock is worked from the toe up.

As a French-Canadian who has lived in older apartments for most of her adult life, I am familiar with the bone-chilling combination of cold weather and hardwood floors. When I was a college student, I wore thick, knitted Afghan socks over another pair of socks to keep my feet warm. With their rough wool and tight stitches, they resembled indoor boots more than socks.

Made from the toe up like their Afghan counterparts, the simplified socks here knit up quickly and can be completed in a weekend. I chose a blend of alpaca and wool soft enough to wear directly against the skin. If your dwelling has hardwood floors, consider adding leather soles—available in many specialty craft stores—to prevent unintentional acrobatics.

TOE
Using the provisional method (see Special Techniques, page 136) and A, CO 6 sts. Work 4 rows St st. Undo waste yarn and place cast-on sts on second dpn, making sure that you have 6 sts (fudge if necessary).

Begin Working in the Round: N1: K3, place marker (pm) for beg of rnd, k3; N2: yo, pick up and knit 1 st on side of strip, yo; N3: k6; N4: yo, pick up and knit 1 st from other side of strip, yo; N1: knit to marker—18 sts.

Increase Round: Inc 1 st at beg and end of N2 and N4 until there are 13 (15, 17) sts on N2 and N4 as follows: *N1: Knit; N2: yo, k1-tbl, k1, k1-tbl, yo; rep from * across N3 and N4, always knitting the yo's of previous rnd tbl—38 (42, 46) sts total. Redistribute sts evenly on needles with marker as beg of rnd (this is important because this is where heel will begin).

FOOT
Work even until toe measures 2½ (2¾, 2¾)" from beg.

Begin Stripe Pattern: Change to B and work even in Stripe patt until foot measures 9¼ (9¾, 10)".

Establish Heel: With waste yarn, k19 (21, 23) sts. Break waste yarn. Slip sts just worked to other end of needle. Beg at marker and using A, knit across sts just knit in waste yarn. The heel will be worked after leg is finished.

LEG
Cont working in Stripe patt until a second B stripe has been knit above heel. Knit 18 rnds A, 6 rnds B, then 6 rnds A. BO all sts loosely.

HEEL
Carefully remove waste yarn and place open sts on 2 needles [19 (21, 23) sts on bottom needle, 18 (20, 22) sts on top needle]. Beg working on top needle, set up heel sts as follows: N1: With A, pick up and knit 1 st tbl, k9 (10, 11); N2: k9 (10, 11), pick up and knit 1 st tbl; N3: pick up and knit 1 st tbl, k9 (10, 11); N4: k10 (11, 12)—40 (44, 48) sts total. Pm for beg of rnd. Knit 1 rnd.

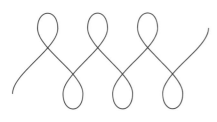

Decrease Rnd: *N1: K2, ssk, knit to end; N2: knit to last 4 sts, k2tog, k2; rep from * across N3 and N4. Cont decreasing in this manner every other rnd twice, then every rnd until 12 sts rem (3 on each needle). K3 on N1, then cut yarn, leaving an 8" tail. Slip sts on N2 to N1, and sts on N3 to N4. Using tail and Kitchener st (see Special Techniques, page 136), graft live sts together.

FINISHING

Embroidery: With yarn needle and B, embroider looped lines (as shown in illustration and photo) by weaving yarn under half-stitches.

CORD AND POMPOMS

Using both colors, make two 12" lengths of twisted cord (see Special Techniques, page 136). Using both colors, make four 1½" diameter pompoms (see Special Techniques, page 136). Attach pompoms to ends of twisted cords. Attach cords to sides of socks with crochet hook.

Weave in all ends. Use tail at beg of heel to close up any "gap." Block to finished measurements.

Tabi Socks

SIZE
To fit women's US shoe size 6–10

FINISHED MEASUREMENTS
Leg length: 6½"
Foot circumference: 8"

YARN
Schachenmayr Regia Silk (55% wool / 25% polyamide / 20% silk; 218 yds / 50 g): 2 balls #02 natural

NEEDLES
One set of five double-pointed needles (dpn) size US 2 (2.5 mm)
Change needle size if necessary to obtain correct gauge.

NOTIONS
Stitch marker, yarn needle, stitch holder, waste yarn

GAUGE
32 sts and 46 rnds = 4" (10 cm) in Stockinette stitch (St st)

ABBREVIATIONS
N1, N2, N3, N4: Needles 1, 2, 3, 4 (N1 and N4 are sole, N2 and N3 are instep)

Although information on knitting in Japan is hard to find, knitwear designer Yoshimi Kihara provides some history on her website (www.knitjapan.co.uk). Many of the old knit objects and garments found in Japan were either imported or made with the technique of *naalbinding* (a single-needle knitting technique similar to darning). Knitting as we know it was brought to Japan by European traders, possibly in the early years of the Edo period (1603–1867). There is even evidence that samurai warriors knit *tabi*—socks with a separation between the big toe and the other toes—to supplement their income at the end of the Edo period, when their influence was waning.

Still a popular Japanese hosiery item today, tabi are worn with all types of thong sandals. While they appear and feel odd to many Westerners at first, they are comfortable to wear once you adjust to them. The socks here echo the lacy knitting patterns favored in contemporary Japan.

LEG
With MC, CO 64 sts. Distribute sts evenly on four dpns; place marker (pm) and join for working in the rnd, being careful not to twists sts. Work Rnds 1 and 2 of Border Chart 4 times, and Rnds 3 and 4 of Border Chart 5 times. Knit 1 rnd, purl 2 rnds.
Establish Leg Pattern: Work Rnds 1–12 of Lace Chart 3 times—leg measures approximately 4½".

HEEL FLAP
Slip sts from second needle to first needle. Working back and forth on these sts only, cont working heel flap as follows:
Row 1 (RS): M1, k2tog, k1, yo, p26, yo, k1, ssk, M1, turn—34 sts.
Row 2: Slip 1, p3, k26, p4.
Row 3: Slip 1 wyib, k2tog, k1, yo, *slip 1 wyib, k1; rep from * to last 4 sts, end yo, k1, ssk, k1.

Row 4: Slip 1, purl to end.
Rep Rows 3–4 15 times more—34 rows completed.

TURN HEEL
Row 1 (RS): Slip 1, k18, ssk, k1, turn.
Row 2: Slip 1, p5, p2tog, p1, turn.
Row 3: Slip 1, k6, ssk, k1, turn.
Cont working in this manner, working 1 additional st before the dec on each row, until 20 sts rem, ending with a WS row.

SHAPE GUSSET
Pick-up rnd: N1: Slip 1 st, k19 across heel flap, then pick up 17 sts along the side of the heel, then pick up a st from the row below the first instep st to prevent a hole; N2 and N3: maintain lace patt as est; N4: pick up a st from the row below the first heel st to prevent a hole, then pick up 17 sts along the side of the heel, then knit the

first 10 sts on N1. Pm for beg of rnd—88 stitches arranged 28–16–16–28.
Rnd 1: N1: Knit to last 3 sts, k2tog, k1; N2 and N3: work Lace patt; N4: K1, ssk, knit to end.
Rnd 2: Work even.
Rep [Rnds 1 and 2] 11 more times—64 sts rem (16 sts on each needle).

FOOT
Work even until foot measures 8" from heel, or 2" short of desired finished length. End Lace patt.

SHAPE TOE (RIGHT FOOT)
Rnd 1: N1: Knit to last 2 sts, k2tog; N2: ssk, knit to end; N3: k6 and place rem 10 sts on holder; using waste yarn and provisional method (see Special Techniques, page 136), CO 6 sts; N4: place first 10 sts on holder, K6. Redistribute sts so that there are 9 sts on N3 and N4—48 sts rem on needles.
Rnds 2, 4, 6, and 8: Knit around.
Rnd 3: N1: Knit to last 2 sts, k2tog; N2: ssk, knit to end; N3: knit to last 4 sts, ssk, k2; N4: k2, k2tog, knit to end—44 sts rem.
Rnd 5: N1: Knit to last 2 sts, k2tog; N2: ssk, knit to end; N3: knit to last 3 sts, ssk, k1; N4: k1, k2tog, knit to end—40 sts rem.
Rnd 7: N1: Knit to last 2 sts, k2tog; N2: ssk, knit to end; N3 and N4: knit—38 sts rem.

Rep [Rnds 7 and 8] 4 more times—
30 sts rem.

Next 4 rnds: N1: *Knit to last 2 sts,
k2tog; N2: ssk, knit to end; rep
from * across N3 and N4—14 sts
rem. K4 on N1. Cut yarn, leaving
an 8" tail.

Slip sts from N4 to N1 and from N2
to N3. Holding N1 and N3 parallel,
graft sts using Kitchener st (see
Special Techniques, page 136). Weave
in ends on inside of sock.

Shape Big Toe: Remove waste yarn
and place base of CO sts on needle—
5 sts. Replace held sts on needles and
distribute so that there are 7 sts on
right front needle (N1), 5 sts on left
front needle (N2), 5 sts on back right
needle (N3), and 8 sts on back left
needle (N4)—25 sts.

Rnd 1: N1: K2, M1, knit to end; N2
and N3: knit; N4: k5, M1, knit to
end—27 sts.

Rnd 2: N1: K2, k2tog, knit to end;
N2 and N3: knit; N4: k4, ssk, knit to
end—25 sts.

Rnds 3, 5, and 7: Knit around.

Rnd 4: N1: K1, k2tog, knit to end;
N2 and N3: knit; N4: k4, ssk, knit to
end—23 sts.

Rnd 6: N1, N2, and N3: Knit. N4: k4,
ssk, knit to end—22 sts.

Cont in St st until toe measures 1½",
or ½" less than desired length.

Next rnd: *N1: Ssk, knit to end; N2:
knit to last 2 sts, k2tog; rep from *
across N3 and N4.
Rep last rnd 2 more times—10 sts rem.
Break yarn, leaving an 8" tail.

Slip sts from N4 to N1 and from N2 to
N3. Holding N1 and N3 parallel, graft
sts using Kitchener st.

SHAPE TOE (LEFT FOOT)
Work as for right foot by reversing
shaping as follows: When foot is
desired length, knit across N1 and
N2 in St st. Re-number needles as
follows: N3 becomes N1, N4 becomes
N2, N1 becomes N3, and N2
becomes N4. Cont as for right foot.

FINISHING
Weave in loose ends.

KEY

- ☐ Knit
- ⊡ Purl
- ⊙ Yo
- ⊠ K2tog
- ⊠ Ssk
- ⊠ Sk2p
- ⊠ K3tog
- ⊠ M1

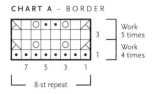

CHART A – BORDER

Work 5 times
Work 4 times

7 5 3 1

8-st repeat

CHART B – LACE

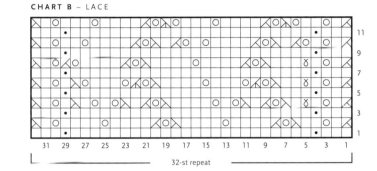

11
9
7
5
3
1

31 29 27 25 23 21 19 17 15 13 11 9 7 5 3 1

32-st repeat

Warm Shawl

FINISHED MEASUREMENTS
Width: approx. 24"
Length: 60" after blocking

YARN
Blue Sky Alpaca & Silk (50% alpaca /
50% silk; 146 yds / 50 g): 5 skeins
#i50 night (A), 2 skeins #i00 slate (B),
and 3 skeins #i13 ice (C)

NEEDLES
One 32" circular (circ) needle size
US 4 (3.5 mm)
Change needle size if necessary to
obtain correct gauge.

NOTIONS
Waste yarn, yarn needle

GAUGE
20 sts and 40 rows = 4" (10 cm) in
Garter st (knit every row) before blocking

In their book *Gossamer Webs*, Galina Khmeleva and Carol R. Noble recount the history of Orenburg lace shawls, magnificent cobweb creations knit in lace and said to date back to the reign of Catherine the Great in early 18th-century Russia. According to legend, an Orenburg craftswoman presented Catherine with an exquisitely worked shawl and, in a fit of cruelty, the empress had the woman blinded so that no one else could have a comparable piece. But the woman's daughter had also learned to make shawls of this quality, and so the tradition continued.

Orenburg knitters still make these shawls, generally for sale, and knit simpler shawls, known as "warm shawls," for themselves. These sturdier pieces usually feature a garter stitch center with lace-patterned borders and are knit of heavier yarn. Despite my admiration for the more elaborate pieces—especially a multicolored version incorporating intarsia—I knew I'd be more likely to use a simpler shawl. Still, my design recalls the multi-colored gossamer through the use of stripes. Knit in a luxurious blend of alpaca and silk, this shawl's ease of construction belies its versatility.

CENTER
With A, waste yarn, and provisional CO method (see Special Techniques, page 136), CO 75 sts. Work even in Garter st for a total of 486 rows (243 ridges)—piece should measure approx 48½" from beg.

FIRST SHORT BORDER
(RS) Change to B. Knit 2 rows. Work Rows 1–10 of Chart A—85 sts. Change to C and work Rows 1–20 of Chart B—105 sts. Knit 1 row. BO knitwise on WS.

SECOND SHORT BORDER
(RS) Remove waste yarn from opposite end and place cast-on sts on needle. Work as for first short border.

LONG BORDERS
(RS) With B, pick up and knit 243 sts from one long side (1 st for each ridge).
Next row (WS): Knit.
Work Rows 1–10 of Chart A—253 sts. Change to C and work Rows 1–20 of Chart B—273 sts. Knit 1 row. BO knitwise on WS.
Rep on opposite side.

FINISHING
Sew border edges together. Weave in loose ends. Block piece to finished measurements.

KEY

Knit on RS, purl on WS.

Purl on RS, knit on WS.

Yo

K2tog

Ssk

Sk2p

CHART A

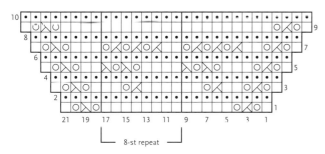

8-st repeat

CHART B

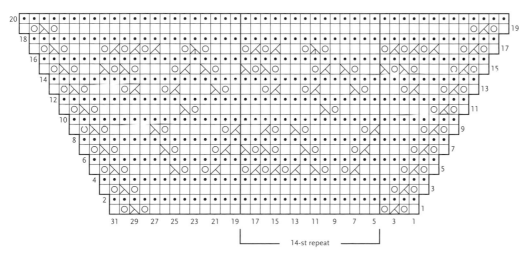

14-st repeat

OBI SCARF

FINISHED MEASUREMENTS
Approximately 7" wide by 66" long

YARN
Mountain Colors Mountain Goat
(55% mohair / 45% wool; 230 yds /
100 g): 3 skeins ruby river

NEEDLES
One pair straight needles size
US 4 (3.5 mm)
Two double-pointed needles (dpn)
size US 4 (3.5 mm)
Change needle size if necessary to
obtain correct gauge.

NOTIONS
Stitch holder, yarn needle, cable
needle (cn)

GAUGE
24 sts and 24 rows = 4" (10 cm) in
pattern after blocking

STITCH PATTERN
See Chart.

NOTE
▸ Place a marker at the beginning
  of the side on which patterning
  is worked; although the scarf is
  reversible, this side will be
  considered the RS.

I don't understand a word of Japanese, yet my knitting library contains many titles in this difficult language. This is not surprising, as Japanese patterns are conveyed with charts and diagrams, and any knitter comfortable reading charts can usually understand them.

In my attempt to knit a scarf suggestive of an *obi*—a reversible sash worn as a belt with the traditional Japanese kimono—I looked for ways to make it attractive on both sides. In the scarf here, the center cable recalls the largely decorative *obijime* cord tied around a woman's *obi*. It is ribbed in order to make it reversible. Similarly, the lace pattern, made up of knit and purl stitches, is different yet equally attractive when viewed from either side.

FIRST HALF
CO 42 sts. Knit 6 rows, then work Rows 1–20 of Chart 10 times; do not turn cable on Row 19 of last repeat. Cut yarn, leaving a 12" tail. Place sts on holder.

SECOND HALF
Work as for first half, but end on Row 19 of last rep (do not turn cable). Slip sts to a dpn, then slip sts from holder to a second dpn. Yarn tails should be at opposite ends of needles.

JOIN ENDS
With RS held tog, BO the two ends tog as follows: *With yarn between needles, slip first st on front needle knitwise, then purl first st on back needle*; psso; rep from * to *, then

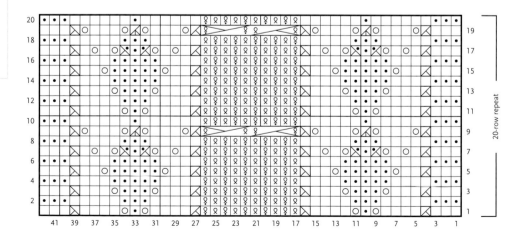

pass the first 2 sts on RH needle over the purled st. Cont in this manner, passing the first 2 sts over the purled st, until 21 sts have been bound off. Turn pieces around to bind off from opposite edge towards the center, using 2nd tail and keeping RS together. BO rem 21 sts, plus the single st at center, in the same manner as before. Cut yarn and fasten off last st.

FINISHING
Weave in loose ends. Block to finished measurements.

KEY

☐	Knit on RS, purl on WS.
⊡	Purl on RS, knit on WS.
⊙	Yo
⊠	K2tog
⊠	Ssk
🧎	K1-tbl on RS, p1-tbl on WS.
🧎	P1-tbl on RS, k1-tbl on WS.
⊠	P2tog
⊠	Ssp
⊠	Sp2p: Slip 1, p2tog, psso.

Slip 5 sts to cn, hold to back, p1-tbl, [k1-tbl, p1-tbl] twice; k1-tbl, [p1-tbl, k1-tbl] twice, from cn.

Slip 5 sts to cn, hold to back, k1-tbl, [p1-tbl, k1-tbl] twice; p1-tbl, [k1-tbl, p1-tbl] twice, from cn.

Faeroese Sweater

SIZES
X-Small (Small, Medium, Large, X-Large, 2X-Large) Shown in size Small

FINISHED MEASUREMENTS
Chest: 35¼ (38¼, 41, 44, 47, 49¾)"

YARN
AmiAmi Medium (100% wool; 219 yds / 100 g): 5 (5, 6, 7, 7, 8) balls #B16 blue (MC), 3 (3, 4, 4, 5, 5) balls #B07 brown (A), 1 (1, 2, 2, 2, 2) ball(s) #B12 green (B), and 1 (1, 2, 2, 2, 2) ball(s) natural (C)

NEEDLES
One each 16" and 32" circular (circ) needles size US 6 (4 mm)
One each 16" and 32" circular needles size US 7 (4.5 mm)
One set of five double-pointed needles (dpn) size US 6 (4 mm)
One set of five double-pointed needles size US 7 (4.5 mm)
Change needle size if necessary to obtain correct gauge.

NOTIONS
Stitch markers (one in contrasting color for beg of rnd), stitch holders, yarn needle

GAUGE
22 sts and 24 rnds = 4" (10 cm) using Stranded Stitch on larger needles

STITCH PATTERN
Knotted Rib
(multiple of 4 sts; 2-rnd rep)
Rnd 1: [K2tog, p2] around.
Rnd 2: [Knit into front and back of next st, p2] around.
Rep Rnds 1 and 2 for Knotted Rib.

The fishermen's sweaters of the Faeroe Islands, a self-governed region of Denmark situated halfway between Scotland and Iceland, rely on the insulating properties of stranded knitting, as the yarn carried along the back of the fabric makes the sweaters warmer and more resistant to the elements. Knitters from the Faeroe Islands, like their Scottish and Nordic cousins, traditionally work in the round from hem to shoulder and then cut down openings for the arms. This is an understandably daunting prospect for many knitters; knitting teacher and author Elizabeth Zimmermann famously prescribed a darkened room and cool washcloth to aid in recovery after the first cut.

This sweater, intended for the more faint of heart, is also knit in the round but as a raglan, so it requires no cuts. Like its Faeroese counterparts, it has no discernable front or back, and thus the elbows and the rest of the sweater wear evenly, as the sweater is put on randomly front to back or back to front every time it is worn. Due to the wide range of colors occurring naturally in locally produced wool, Faeroese knitters traditionally work with undyed yarns. My contemporary sweater is just as colorful, but the colors I chose have not yet been found on the back of a sheep.

BODY

Lower Rib: With smaller 32" circ needle and MC, CO 204 (220, 236, 252, 268, 284) sts. Place marker (pm) for beg of rnd and join, being careful not to twist sts. Work in Knotted Rib for

NOTES
▸ Body and Sleeves are worked in the round to the underarm, joined, then worked in the round to the neck. *All pieces must end on same round of Chart prior to joining.*
▸ When working colorwork on Sleeves and Raglan Yoke, work stitches adjacent to markers in MC on all rounds.

4", ending on Rnd 2. Knit 1 rnd, decreasing 10 sts evenly around—194 (210, 226, 242, 258, 274) sts rem.
Begin Body Pattern: Change to larger 32" circ needle, and work Rnds 1–6 of Chart B, beginning where indicated, until piece measures 11¼ (11½, 11¾, 12, 12¼, 12½)" from beg, ending 2 (3, 4, 5, 6, 7) sts before marker on last rnd.
Divide for Front and Back: Cont Chart B, k4 (6, 8, 10, 12, 14) sts and place on holder for underarm, k93 (99, 105, 111, 117, 123), k4 (6, 8, 10, 12, 14) sts and place on holder for underarm, knit to end—93 (99, 105, 111, 117, 123) sts each for Front and Back. Do not break yarn. Set aside.

SLEEVES (make 2)
Cuff: With smaller dpns and MC, CO 64 (64, 64, 72, 72, 72) sts. Arrange evenly across 4 needles, pm, and join, being careful not to twist sts. Work in Knotted Rib for 5", ending with Rnd 2. Knit 1 rnd, decreasing 10 (8, 6, 12, 10, 8) sts evenly around—54 (56, 58, 60, 62, 64) sts rem.

Shape Sleeve: Change to larger dpns and work Rnds 1–6 of Chart A twice, then rep Rnds 1–6 of Chart B for rest of Sleeve. AT THE SAME TIME, inc 2 sts every 6 rnds 7 (0, 0, 0, 0, 0) times, every 5 rnds 5 (14, 9, 4, 0, 0) times, every 4 rnds 0 (0, 7, 14, 19, 16) times, and every 3 rnds 0 (0, 0, 0, 1, 6) time(s) as follows: K1, M1-R, work in patt to last st, M1-L, k1 (see Notes), working new sts in patt as est—78 (84, 90, 96, 102, 108) sts. Work even until Sleeve measures 16½ (17, 17½, 18, 18½, 19)" from beg (ending on same rnd as for Body); work last rnd to 2 (3, 4, 5, 6, 7) sts before marker.

Next rnd: K4 (6, 8, 10, 12, 14) sts and place on holder for underarm, knit to end—74 (78, 82, 86, 90, 94) sts rem. Break yarn and set aside.

YOKE
Using yarn and needle from Body and cont in patt as est, k74 (78, 82, 86, 90, 94) left Sleeve sts, pm, k93 (99, 105, 111, 117, 123) Front sts, pm, k74 (78, 82, 86, 90, 94) right Sleeve sts, pm, k93 (99, 105, 111, 117, 123) Back sts, pm for beg of rnd—334 (354, 374, 394, 414, 434) sts.

Shape Raglan Yoke: Dec 2 sts at each raglan line (see Notes) on 2 out of

every 3 rnds 16 (17, 18, 19, 20, 21) times as follows:
Rnds 1 and 2: *Ssk, work in patt to 2 sts before next marker, k2tog; rep from * 3 more times—8 sts dec'd on each rnd.
Rnd 3: Knit—78 (82, 86, 90, 94, 98) sts rem. If necessary, work even until yoke measures approx 8 (8½, 9, 9½, 10, 10½)" from underarm, ending with Rnd 3 or 6 of Chart B.

TURTLENECK

Cont with MC only, inc 2 sts evenly on next rnd—80 (84, 88, 92, 96, 100) sts. Change to smaller 16" circ needle and purl 1 rnd, removing all markers except at beg of rnd. Work Knotted Rib for 2", ending with Rnd 2.

Reverse Work for Fold Over Collar:
Rnd 1: Knit to marker, yo, turn.
Rnd 2: Work Rnd 1 of Knotted Rib to last st; slip this last st and remove marker, then purl it together with yo next to it. Replace marker and cont with Knotted Rib for 5" more, ending with Rnd 2. BO loosely in rib.

FINISHING

Graft underarm sts using Kitchener st (see Special Techniques, page 136). Weave in loose ends. Block to finished measurements.

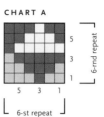

CHART A

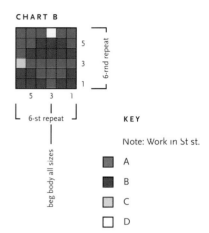

CHART B

KEY

Note: Work in St st.

- ■ A
- ■ B
- ▨ C
- □ D

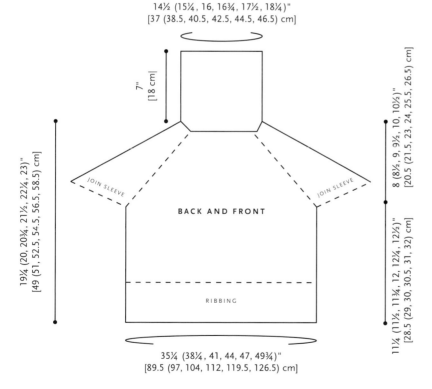

14½ (15¼, 16, 16¾, 17½, 18¼)"
[37 (38.5, 40.5, 42.5, 44.5, 46.5) cm]

7"
[18 cm]

19¼ (20, 20¾, 21½, 22¼, 23)"
[49 (51, 52.5, 54.5, 56.5, 58.5) cm]

JOIN SLEEVE   JOIN SLEEVE

BACK AND FRONT

RIBBING

8 (8½, 9, 9½, 10, 10½)"
[20.5 (21.5, 23, 24, 25.5, 26.5) cm]

11¼ (11½, 11¾, 12, 12¼, 12½)"
[28.5 (29, 30, 30.5, 31, 32) cm]

35¼ (38¼, 41, 44, 47, 49¾)"
[89.5 (97, 104, 112, 119.5, 126.5) cm]

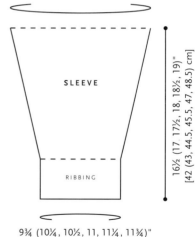

14¼ (15¼, 16¼, 17½, 18½, 19¾)"
[36.5 (38.5, 41.5, 44.5, 47, 50) cm]

SLEEVE

RIBBING

16½ (17, 17½, 18, 18½, 19)"
[42 (43, 44.5, 45.5, 47, 48.5) cm]

9¾ (10¼, 10½, 11, 11¼, 11¾)"
[25 (26, 26.5, 27.5, 28.5, 30) cm]

LATVIAN FINGERLESS MITTS

FINISHED MEASUREMENTS
Circumference: 7½"
Length: 7"

YARN
Reynolds Whiskey (100% wool;
195 yds / 50 g): 1 ball each #102
orange (A), #53 teal (B), #101 light
orange (C), #16 burgundy (D), and
#103 green (E)

NEEDLES
One set of five double-pointed
needles (dpn) size US 0 (2 mm)
Change needle size if necessary to
obtain correct gauge.

NOTIONS
Stitch markers, stitch holder, yarn
needle

GAUGE
34 sts and 36 rnds = 4" (10 cm) over
Stranded Stockinette st

NOTE
▶ When increasing stitches for thumb
gusset, make one stitch (M1) by
picking up the strand in rnd below
(pick up strand that is color of M1
symbol on Chart) and knitting it
through the back loop, using the
contrasting color yarn.

Soon after learning to knit in 2000, I began to seek out books and magazines on the subject. It was then that I came across *Interweave Knits* magazine and its editor, Melanie Falick. My interest piqued, I ordered, sight unseen, a copy of her book *Knitting in America*.

Those of you familiar with the book know why my copy is practically falling apart. Not only did it inspire me to knit more, it also acquainted me with many passionate, accomplished knitters, including Lizbeth Upitis, whose study of Latvian mittens fascinates me to this day. In her book *Latvian Mittens*, she writes of the historical and cultural role of mittens in this country on the Baltic Sea, recounting how Latvian girls knitted them for their dowries, filling entire chests to lessen the number of cattle their families had to supply to seal proposals of marriage. Ms. Upitis's many intricate pattern charts were so beautiful that I had trouble choosing among them for my mitten interpretation. In the end, I adapted two patterns from the district of Vidzeme to my fingerless mitts, basing my color choices on the gorgeous mittens in her collection.

HEM FACING AND CUFF
With A, CO 64 sts. Distribute sts evenly on 4 dpns; place marker (pm) and join for working in the rnd, being careful not to twist sts. Knit 6 rnds, purl 1 rnd (turning rnd), knit 2 rnds. Work Rnds 1–24 of Cuff Chart—piece measures approx 3¾" from beg.

HAND AND THUMB GUSSET
Working Rnds 25–32 of Hand Chart 4 times, shape thumb gusset as follows:
Rnd 1: Work 31 sts in colorwork as charted, pm; with D, (k1, yo, k1) in next stitch, pm, and starting at beg of 8-st rep, work in colorwork as charted to end of rnd.
Rnds 2–17: Work Thumb Gusset Chart between markers, increasing as indicated on Chart.

Work even in patt as est until thumb gusset measures 2½".

TOP OF HAND
Work in patt as est, remove marker; k19 gusset sts in patt as est and place these on waste yarn or holder; remove marker; work in patt as est to end of rnd. Cont working Hand Chart until Rnds 25–32 have been repeated 4 times—mitt measures approx 7¼" from beg. Change to E and knit 1 rnd, purl 1 rnd. Change to B and knit 1 rnd. BO all sts purlwise.

TOP OF THUMB
Slip Thumb sts back to dpns. With E, pick up and knit 1 st from Hand to close gap at join, then knit to end of

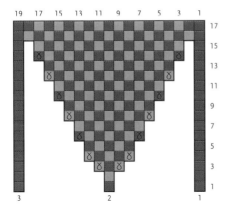

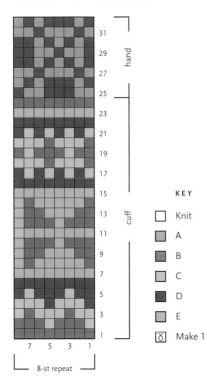

KEY

☐	Knit
▨	A
▩	B
▨	C
■	D
▨	E
⊗	Make 1

rnd—20 sts. Purl 1 rnd. Change to B, and knit 1 rnd. BO all sts purlwise.

FINISHING

Weave in loose ends. Fold hem to WS at turning rnd. With yarn needle and A, sew facing to the WS. Wash and block.

WOOLEN GLOVES

FINISHED MEASUREMENTS
Palm circumference: 7"
Length from base of thumb: 8½"

YARN
Reynolds Whiskey (100% wool;
195 yds / 50 g): 2 balls #053 teal

NEEDLES
One set of five double-pointed
needles (dpn) size US 3 (3.25 mm)
Change needle size if necessary to
obtain correct gauge.

NOTIONS
Stitch markers (one in contrasting
color for beg of rnd), waste yarn or
stitch holders, yarn needle

GAUGE
30 sts and 38 rows = 4" (10 cm) in
Stockinette stitch (St st)

NOTES
▸ Stitches picked up at base of fingers
are *not knit* (i.e. not "pick up and
knit"); instead, pick existing loops
with tip of RH needle and transfer
them to LH needle.

Meant as under-gloves for the Latvian fingerless mitts on page 96, these opera-length gloves recall Icelandic lace-patterned wrist warmers. Iceland's long history of knitting dates back to the 16th century; the country is most famous for its circular yoke sweaters. However, a tradition of lace knitting has also existed since the late 19th century, when Iceland began to import foreign publications featuring lace patterns. Among the items knit in this style were wrist warmers, worn by both men and women, which I have adapted to a design for long, lacy gloves. As any northern dweller will tell you, long gloves are not only elegant but practical for keeping every inch of your wrist covered, no matter the length or width of your coat sleeves.

CUFF
CO 60 sts. Distribute evenly on four dpns; place marker (pm) for beg of rnd, and join, being careful not to twist sts. Purl 1 rnd, knit 1 rnd, purl 1 rnd.

Lower Cuff Pattern:
Rnds 1 and 3: [K1, yo, k2, ssk, k2tog, k2, yo, k1] around.
Rnds 2 and 4: Knit.
Rnd 5: [P1, yo, p2, ssp, p2tog, p2, yo, p1] around.
Rnd 6: Purl.
Rep [Rnds 1–6] until cuff measures approx 4½".
Dec rnd: [K1, yo, k1, sssk, k3tog, k1, yo, k1] around—48 sts. Knit 1 rnd.
Upper Cuff Pattern:
Rnd 1: [P1, yo, p1, ssp, p2tog, p1, yo, p1] around.
Rnd 2: Purl.
Rnds 3 and 5: [K1, yo, k1, ssk, k2tog, k1, yo, k1] around.
Rnds 4 and 6: Knit.
Rep [Rnds 1–6] until cuff measures approx 7", then work [Rnds 1–2] once more. Work even in St st for 1½",

placing markers on last rnd as follows: K23, pm, k2, pm, knit to end of rnd.

THUMB GUSSET
Inc 1 st after first marker and before second marker on next rnd, then every 4 rnds twice, then every other rnd 6 times as follows: Knit to marker, slip marker (sm), M1-R, knit to marker, M1-L, sm, knit to end of rnd—66 sts. Work even until thumb gusset measures 2¾".

UPPER PALM
K23, place next 20 sts on waste yarn or holder for thumb, CO 4 sts, knit to end—50 sts. Work even for 1".

LITTLE FINGER
K5, place next 40 sts on waste yarn or holder, CO 4 sts, k5—14 sts. Work even on these 14 sts for approx 2¼".
Decrease for Tip:
Rnd 1: [K2tog] 7 times—7 sts rem.
Rnd 2: [K2tog] 3 times, k1—4 sts rem.
Cut yarn, thread though rem sts, and pull tight.

Replace 40 held sts on needles; pick up 2 sts at base of little finger and transfer to LH needle (see Notes); re-attach yarn and k1, k2tog, knit to last st and slip it to LH needle; pick up 2 additional sts from little finger, then replace slipped st to RH needle, ssk, k1—42 sts rem. Pm for beg of rnd. Knit 4 rnds.

RING FINGER
K8, place next 26 sts on holder, CO 4 sts, k8—20 sts.
Next rnd: [K2tog, k6, ssk] twice—16 sts rem.
Work even until finger measures approx 2¾".
Decrease for Tip: *[K2tog] around—8 sts rem. Rep from * once more—4 sts rem. Cut yarn, thread through rem sts, and pull tight.

MIDDLE FINGER
Replace next 8 held sts, re-attach yarn and knit the 8 sts, CO 4 sts, replace last 8 held sts and knit them, then pick up 4 sts from base of ring finger so that last 2 sts picked up are on LH needle—24 sts. Pm for beg of rnd between the 4 picked up sts.
Rnd 1: [K1, k2tog, k6, ssk, k1] twice—20 sts rem.
Rnd 2: [K2tog, k6, ssk] twice—16 sts rem.
Work even until finger measures approx 3". Decrease tip as for ring finger.

INDEX FINGER
Replace rem 10 held sts, and pick up 6 sts so that last 3 sts picked up from base of middle finger are on LH needle—16 sts. Pm for beg of rnd between the 4 picked-up sts. Re-attach yarn.
Next Rnd: K1, k2tog, knit to last 3 sts, ssk, k1—14 sts rem.
Work even until finger measures approx 2¾". Decrease tip as for little finger.

THUMB
Replace 20 held thumb sts, and pick up 6 sts from base so that last 3 sts picked up from side of palm are on LH needle—26 sts. Pm for beg of rnd between the 6 picked-up sts.
Next rnd: *K2, k2tog, k5, ssk, k2; rep from * once more—22 sts rem.
Work even until thumb measures approx 2".

Decrease for Tip:
Rnd 1: [K2tog] around—11 sts rem.
Rnd 2: [K2tog] 5 times, k1—6 sts rem.
Rnd 3: [K2tog] around—3 sts rem.
Cut yarn, thread through rem sts, and pull tight.

FINISHING
Weave in loose ends. Block to finished measurements.

GIANT YOKE PONCHO

FINISHED MEASUREMENTS
Neck circumference: 16"
Lower edge circumference: 96"
Length: 33¾"

YARN
Brown Sheep Lamb's Pride
Superwash Worsted (100% washable
wool; 200 yds / 100 g): 6 balls #SW40
combustion grey

NEEDLES
One each 16" and 32" circular (circ)
needles size US 10 (6 mm)
Change needle size if necessary to
obtain correct gauge.

NOTIONS
18 stitch markers (one in contrasting
color for beg of rnd), coiless safety
pin, yarn needle

GAUGE
18 sts and 26 rows = 4" (10 cm) in
Fluted Rib

STITCH PATTERN
Fluted Rib (multiple of 4 sts;
2-rnd rep)
Rnd 1: [K1, p1, k2] around.
Rnd 2: [P3, k1] around.
Rep Rnds 1 and 2 for Fluted Rib.

NOTE
▸ Change to shorter needle when
  necessary.

The poncho, originally a cloak made from a simple blanket with a slit for the head, is thought to have originated in South America, although variations with different names can be traced back to Roman times. In North America, ponchos are often associated with the hippie image, but in designing this one, I was interested in referencing the genius of Claire McCardell, known to many as the mother of American sportswear. A pioneering spirit, McCardell created garments out of humble fabrics such as wool jersey, and drew upon her knowledge of global fashion history to make them multifunctional. Often cut oversized, McCardell's designs frequently called for straps and belts to enable the wearer to arrange the folds upon her body in a stylish yet comfortable manner.

In the same spirit, I used a straightforward wool to knit a giant yoke with shaping as its only embellishment. As the decreases occur all around the piece, there isn't a right or wrong way to wear it. I later made a sweater for my young daughter using a variation of this pattern, and can happily report that no one ever noticed her sweater being back to front—or inside out, for that matter.

BODY
With longer needle, CO 432 sts. Place marker (pm) for beg of rnd and join, being careful not to twist sts. Work in Fluted Rib until piece measures 2¾". Next rnd: *K24, pm; rep from * around—17 new markers placed.

SHAPE TOP
Dec 2 sts before each marker on next rnd, then every 18 rnds 4 times, every 16 rnds twice, then every 12 rnds 3 times as follows: *Work in patt as est to 3 sts before marker, k3tog, slip marker; rep from * around—72 sts rem. Poncho measures approx 24¼".

COLLAR
Place coiless safety pin or other removable marker in fabric to mark beg of collar. Work even until collar measures 9½", removing all markers except beg-of-rnd marker on first rnd. BO all sts loosely in patt.

FINISHING
Weave in all ends. Block to finished measurements.

The advent of leisure time and the popularity of sporting activities have had a far-reaching influence on the clothes we wear, abolishing restrictive styles and contributing to the development of new fibers and new silhouettes. Until the early 20th century, if a woman chose to partake in physical activity, she had to do so in traditional dress—which typically included restrictive garments such as corsets and voluminous, heavy skirts. As sport for women became more popular, fashions became more streamlined, and the heavy layers were shed in favor of easy movement. Bloomers—loose pants worn under skirts—eventually became the norm. And while the trend toward movability eventually led to the development of stretchy fibers such as polyester, rayon, and Lycra, knitwear fit the bill in the meantime, its flexible nature being ideal for movement as well as style.

I've taken historic sporting wear designs into the 21st century by casting them in modern colorways and silhouettes, or by transforming traditional garments with current details. A 19th-century Norwegian sweater becomes a hoodie, a 1970s skateboarding ensemble is softened into a feminine, layered look, a fishermen's gansey becomes a zippered sport vest, and an early 20th-century bathing costume evolves into a halter top.

THRILL SEEKERS

Bicycle Socks

SIZE
To fit women's US shoe size 6–10

FINISHED MEASUREMENTS
Leg length: 8½"
Foot circumference: 8"

YARN
Schoeller + Stahl Fortissima Socka
(75% wool / 25% polyamide;
229 yds / 50 g): 3 balls (MC); 1 ball
each (A), (B), and (C)
Socks with Attached Fancy Tops and
worked in Eyelet Rib shown in #1040
navy (MC), #1006 green (A), #1005
turquoise (B), and #1001 white (C)
Socks with Detachable Fancy Tops and
worked in Graphic Rib shown in #1058
flannel gray (MC), #1010 red (A), #1008
orange (B), and #1007 yellow (C)

NEEDLES
One set of five double-pointed needles
(dpn) size US 0 (2 mm)
Change needle size if necessary to
obtain correct gauge.

NOTIONS
Stitch markers (one in contrasting
color to mark beg of rnd), yarn needle

GAUGE
34 sts and 46 rnds = 4" (10 cm) in
Stockinette stitch (St st)

ABBREVIATIONS
N1, N2, N3, N4 = Needles 1, 2, 3, 4
(N1 and N4 are sole, N2 and N3
are instep)

STITCH PATTERNS
Graphic Rib (multiple of 6 sts; 1-rnd rep)
Rnd 1: *P3, k1-tbl, k1, k1-tbl; rep from
* around.
Rep this rnd for Graphic Rib.

As bicycling grew in popularity at the beginning of the 20th century, so did new styles of clothing adapted to the sport. Men wore knickers and modish socks with decorative tops. As only the uppermost band of these socks was patterned, knitters soon figured out there was no need to knit a full sock every time they wanted a fresh look. Instead, they knit gaily patterned bands that slipped over the tops of socks.

In this tradition, I offer a sock pattern with matching multicolored band, plus a playful striped sock pattern to help use up the leftover yarn. Read the note for the striped sock pattern to learn knitting expert and designer Mona Schmidt's trick for almost-jogless side "seams."

Eyelet Rib (multiple of 6 sts; 8-rnd rep)
Rnd 1 and all odd-numbered rnds: *P3, k3;
rep from * around.
Rnds 2 and 6: *P3, k3; rep from * around.
Rnd 4: *P3, k2tog, yo, k1; rep from * around.
Rnd 8: *P3, k1, yo, ssk; rep from * around.
Rep Rnds 1–8 for Eyelet Rib.

NOTE
▷ This pattern includes several variations:
simple socks with separate fancy tops,
or with fancy tops folded over or not.
You also have the choice of working either
Graphic Rib or Eyelet Rib. The pattern
begins with the Fancy Tops; if you'd like
to omit these, cast on 78 sts with MC
and go directly to the paragraph labeled
"All Styles."

SOCKS SHOWN
Striped sock in green, turquoise, and
white; navy sock with unfolded Fancy Top;
striped sock in red, orange, and yellow;
flannel grey sock with Detachable Fancy
Top band (left to right)

Fancy Top Version

LEG
With MC, CO 84 sts. Arrange sts on
four dpns as follows: 25–26–16–17;
place marker (pm) and join, being
careful not to twists sts.
Rnds 1 and 2: *P1-tbl, k1-tbl; rep
from * around.
Work 4 rnds of Graphic Rib.
Knit 1 rnd, purl 2 rnds.
Work Fancy Chart for 24 rows. Purl 2
rnds. Work Version 1, 2, or 3 as desired.

Version 1: Detachable Fancy Top band
Knit 1 rnd. Work 4 rnds of Graphic Rib.
Next 2 rnds: *P1-tbl, k1-tbl; rep from *
around. BO all sts.
Beg accompanying Sock by casting
on 78 sts, and go to paragraph labeled
"All Styles."

Version 2: Socks with fold-over Fancy
Tops (not shown)
Next rnd: *K12, k2tog; rep from * 5
more times—78 sts rem. With yarn in
front, slip both the marker and the first
st to RH needle; bring yarn to back of

work, and replace both st and marker on LH needle. Turn work inside out, reversing the direction of knitting.

Next rnd: *P3, k1-tbl, k1, k1-tbl; rep from * to last 6 sts, end p3, k1-tbl, k1—1

FANCY CHART

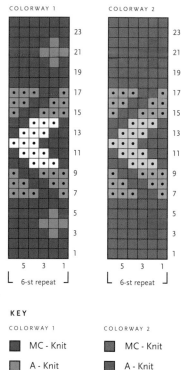

COLORWAY 1

COLORWAY 2

23 21 19 17 15 13 11 9 7 5 3 1

5 3 1
6-st repeat

KEY

COLORWAY 1

- ■ MC - Knit
- ▨ A - Knit
- ▣ B - Purl
- ▢ C - Purl

COLORWAY 2

- ▨ MC - Knit
- ■ A - Knit
- ▣ B - Purl
- ▣ C - Purl

wrapped st remains; lift wrap over needle and knit it together with the last st. Go to paragraph labeled "All Styles."

Version 3: Socks with unfolded Fancy Tops

Next rnd: *K12, k2tog; rep from * 5 more times—78 sts rem.
Go to paragraph labeled "All Styles."

ALL STYLES

Work 12 rnds in either Graphic Rib or Eyelet Rib, as desired. On last rnd, work 21 sts, pm, work 3 sts, pm, work to end of rnd.

Dec 2 sts at center back every 4 rnds 6 times as follows: Work in patt to 2 sts before first marker, p2tog, work to next marker, ssp, work in patt to end of rnd—66 sts rem.

Arrange sts on four dpns as follows: 16–17–16–17. Work even until leg measures 8½" from beg.

HEEL FLAP

Slip sts from second needle to first needle—33 sts on needle. Working back and forth on these sts using A only, work 2 rows in St st. Cont working heel flap as follows:

Row 1 (RS): *Slip 1 wyib, k1; rep from * to last st, end k1.

Row 2: Slip 1, purl to end.

Rep these 2 rows 14 more times.

TURN HEEL

Row 1 (RS): Slip 1, k17, ssk, k1, turn.
Row 2: Slip 1, p4, p2tog, p1, turn.
Row 3: Slip 1, k5, ssk, k1, turn.

Cont working in this manner, working 1 additional st before the decrease on each row, until 19 sts rem, ending with a WS row.

SHAPE GUSSET

Change to MC.

Pick-up rnd: N1: Slip 1, k18 across heel flap, then pick up and knit 17 sts along the side of the heel, then pick up a st from the row below the first instep st to prevent a hole; N2 and N3: maintain patt as est; N4: pick up a st from the row below the first heel st to prevent a hole, then pick up 17 sts along the side of the heel, then knit the first 10 sts on N1; pm for beg of rnd—88 stitches arranged 27–16–17–28.

Rnd 1: N1: Knit to last 3 sts, k2tog, k1; N2 and N3: work in patt as est; N4: k1, ssk, knit to end.

Rnd 2: Work even.

Rep [Rnds 1 and 2] 10 more times— 66 sts rem.

FOOT

Work even until foot measures 7½" from heel or 2½" short of desired finished length. Change to A. Knit 6 rnds.

SHAPE TOE

Rnd 1: *N1: Knit to last 3 sts, k2tog, k1; N2: k1, ssk, knit to end; rep from *— across N3 and N4 62 sts rem.

Rnd 2: Knit around.

Rep [Rnds 1 and 2] 7 more times— 34 sts rem.

Rep [Rnd 1] 4 times—18 sts rem. K4 on N1. Break yarn, leaving an 8" tail.

FINISHING

Slip sts from N4 to N1 and from N2 to N3—9 sts on each needle. Holding N1 and N3 parallel, graft sts using Kitchener st (see Special Techniques, page 136). Weave in ends on inside of sock.

Striped Version

SIZE
To fit women's US shoe size 6–10

FINISHED MEASUREMENTS
Leg length: 7½"
Foot circumference: 8"

YARN
Schoeller + Stahl Fortissima
Socka (75% wool / 25% polyamide;
229 yds / 50 g): 1 ball each (MC), (A),
(B), and (C)
Colorway 1: #1040 navy (MC), #1006
green (A), #1005 turquoise (B),
#1001 white (C); Colorway 2: #1058
flannel gray (MC), #1010 red (A),
#1008 orange (B), #1007 yellow (C)

NEEDLES
One set of five double-pointed
needles (dpn) size US 0 (2 mm)
Change needle size if necessary to
obtain correct gauge.

NOTIONS
Stitch marker, yarn needle

GAUGE
34 sts and 46 rnds = 4" (10 cm) in
Stockinette stitch (St st)

ABBREVIATIONS
N1, N2, N3, N4 = Needles 1, 2, 3, 4
(N1 and N4 are sole, N2 and N3
are instep)

STITCH PATTERNS
Graphic Rib
(multiple of 6 sts; 1-rnd rep)
Rnd 1: *P3, k1-tbl, k1, k1-tbl; rep from
* around.
Rep this rnd for Graphic Rib.

Stripe Pattern
Work 2 rnds A, 2 rnds B, 1 rnd C.
Rep these 5 rnds for Stripe Pattern.

LEG

With MC, CO 66 sts. Arrange sts on
four dpns as follows: 16–17–16–17.
Place marker (pm) and join, being
careful not to twists sts.
Rnds 1 and 2: [P1-tbl, k1-tbl] around.
Rnds 3–14: Work in Graphic Rib.
Purl 1 rnd. Break MC and change
to Stripe Pattern. Work even until
leg measures 7½" from beg, ending
with C.

HEEL FLAP

Slip sts from second needle to first
needle—33 sts on needle. Working
back and forth on these sts using MC
only, work 2 rows in St st. Cont
working heel flap as follows:
Row 1 (RS): *Slip 1 wyib, k1; rep
from * to last st, end k1.
Row 2: Slip 1, purl to end.
Rep these 2 rows 14 more times.

TURN HEEL

Row 1 (RS): Slip 1, k17, ssk, k1, turn.
Row 2: Slip 1, p4, p2tog, p1, turn.
Row 3: Slip 1, k5, ssk, k1, turn.
Cont working in this manner,
working 1 additional st before the
decrease on each row, until 19 sts
rem, ending with a WS row.

NOTE
To make the jog at the "side seam" less
visible and keep the stitches at the
beginning of the round even, use
Mona's trick of keeping the yarns in
order and always picking the new yarn
from under the other 2 yarns.

SHAPE GUSSET

Break MC and cont in Stripe Pattern as
est, beg with A.
Pick-up rnd: N1: Slip 1, k18 across
heel flap, then pick up and knit 17 sts
along the side of the heel, then pick up
a st from the row below the first instep
st to prevent a hole; N2 and N3: knit;
N4: pick up a st from the row below
the first heel st to prevent a hole, then
pick up 17 sts along the side of the
heel, then knit the first 10 sts on N1;
pm for beg of rnd—88 sts arranged
27–16–17–28.
Rnd 1: N1: Knit to last 3 sts, k2tog,
k1; N2 and N3: knit; N4: k1, ssk, knit
to end.
Rnd 2: Knit around.
Rep [Rnds 1 and 2] 10 more times—
66 sts rem.

FOOT

Work even until foot measures 7½"
from heel, or 2½" short of desired
finished length. Change to MC.
Knit 6 rnds.

SHAPE TOE

Rnd 1: *N1: Knit to last 3 sts, k2tog,
k1; N2: k1, ssk, knit to end; rep from *
across N3 and N4—62 sts rem.
Rnd 2: Knit around.
Rep [Rnds 1 and 2] 7 more times—
34 sts rem.
Rep [Rnd 1] 4 times—18 sts rem.
K4 on N1.
Break yarn, leaving an 8" tail.

FINISHING

Slip sts from N4 to N1 and from N2
to N3—9 sts on each needle. Holding
N1 and N3 parallel, graft sts using
Kitchener st (see Special Techniques,
page 136). Weave in ends on inside
of sock.

FAIR ISLE CARDIGAN

SIZES
X-Small (Small, Medium, Large,
X-Large, 2X-Large) Shown in Small

FINISHED MEASUREMENTS
Chest: 37 (40, 43, 46, 49, 52)"
(closed)

YARN
Jamieson & Smith 2 Ply Jumper
Weight (100% Shetland wool;
125 yds / 25 g): 3 (3, 4, 4, 4, 5) balls of
#FC66 charcoal (A); 2 (2, 3, 3, 3, 3)
balls each of #FC9 lilac (B), #83 olive
(C), #FC48 cobalt (D), #43 magenta
(E), #133 dark fuchsia (F), #FC56
purple (G), #FC13 warm brown (H),
#33 light blue (I), #1A off white (J),
#61 camel (K), and #203 silver gray (L)

NEEDLES
One each 16" and 32" circular (circ)
needles size US 3 (3.25 mm)
One set of five double-pointed
needles (dpn) size US 3 (3.25 mm)
Change needle size if necessary to
obtain correct gauge.

NOTIONS
Stitch markers, yarn needle, eleven
½" buttons

GAUGE
32 sts and 33 rows = 4" (10 cm) in
Stranded Stockinette st (St st)

NOTES
- Read all instructions through
completely before beginning a piece
or section; changes in colorwork
and shaping occur simultaneously.
- It is important that you work the
number of rounds specified in the
text to armhole shaping for both Body
and Sleeves so that the patterning
matches up. If you make revisions for
desired length, make sure that you make
armhole bind-offs on the same round for
all pieces.
- Steek sts are worked in Stranded Knitting
and may be worked as vertical stripes or
in a checkerboard pattern.
- After steek is established, those sts are
not included in stitch counts.

Fair Isle sweaters became popular in Great Britain in the 1920s, after the young Prince of Wales was photographed teeing off on the golf links at St Andrews in a handsome cardigan he had received as a wedding gift. Advertised in *Punch* magazine as the perfect sportswear, these brightly colored sweaters from the Shetlands fitted the spirit of the Jazz Age perfectly. As women were increasingly becoming involved in active sports, the sweaters were adopted by both sexes, and they have remained a classic fashion item ever since.

The Fair Isle stranded knitting technique builds carefully designed patterns in horizontal bands, using two colors in each row and as many as twelve or more in a garment. My design combines classic Fair Isle techniques with a slim silhouette and set-in sleeves. The Jazz Age's daring use of color is reflected here in a combination of neutrals with brighter tones of fuchsia, cobalt, and lavender.

BODY
Using longer circ needle and A, CO 298 (322, 346, 370, 394, 418) sts. Place marker (pm) for beg of rnd and join, being careful not to twist sts.
Establish Rib and Steek: Work 288 (312, 336, 360, 384, 408) sts in Ribbing (see Ribbing Chart), pm, k10 sts in steek pattern (see Notes and Special Techniques, page 136). Complete Rnds 2–10 of Ribbing Chart, increasing 1 st on last rnd—289 (313, 337, 361, 385, 409) non-steek sts (see Notes).
Establish Fair Isle Pattern: Work Rnds 1–48 of Peerie Chart 2 (2, 3, 3, 3, 3) times and Rnds 1–43 (1–47, 1–3, 1–7, 1–11, 1–15) once more.

Note: Armhole and neck shaping occur at the same time that color work pattern changes; please read the following section all the way through before continuing.

SHAPE ARMHOLES AND FRONT NECK
Rnd 1: Working in color patt, k60 (65, 70, 75, 80, 85) Front sts, BO 17 (19, 21, 23, 25, 27) underarm sts, k135 (145, 155, 165, 175, 185) Back sts, BO 17 (19, 21, 23, 25, 27) sts, knit to end.

Rnd 2: K58 (63, 68, 73, 78, 83), ssk, pm, CO 10 sts for right armhole steek, pm, k2tog, k131 (141, 151, 161, 171, 181), ssk, pm, CO 10 sts for left armhole steek, pm, k2tog, knit to end—59 (64, 69, 74, 79, 84) sts each Front, 133 (143, 153, 163, 173, 183) Back sts. Cont in patt as est and, maintaining all steeks, dec 1 st at each armhole edge every rnd 7 (9, 11, 13, 15, 17) times, every other rnd 3 times, and every 4 rnds twice as follows: *Knit to 2 sts before marker, ssk, slip marker (sm), work steek, sm, k2tog, rep from * once more, knit to end of rnd—12 (14, 16, 18, 20, 22) sts decreased at each marker and 109 (115, 121, 127, 133, 139) Back sts rem.

AT THE SAME TIME, when armholes measure 1¼", begin neck shaping,

decreasing 1 st at neck edge on next rnd, then every other rnd 22 (23, 24, 25, 26, 27) times as follows: k2tog, work in patt as est to last 2 sts of rnd, ssk—24 (26, 28, 30, 32, 34) sts rem for each front shoulder.

AT THE SAME TIME, when 1 (2, 2, 2, 2, 2) full (7-rnd) Peerie bands have been completed following the beg of armhole, work Rnds 1–19 of Yoke Chart. Cont to work Peerie Chart, beg with the next band in sequence. Work even until armholes measure 6 (6½, 7, 7½, 8, 8½)". BO all sts.

SLEEVES (make 2)

Using dpns and A, CO 80 (84, 88, 92, 96, 100) sts. Distribute evenly on needles, pm for beg of rnd, and join, being careful not to twist sts. (Change to shorter circ needle when there are enough sts.)

Establish Rib: Work Rnds 1–10 of Ribbing Chart, increasing 1 st on last rnd—81 (85, 89, 93, 97, 101) sts.

Establish Fair Isle Pattern: Taking care to center pattern (see Special Techniques, page 136), work Rnds 17–48 of Peerie Chart once, Rnds 1–48 1 (1, 2, 2, 2, 2) time(s) and Rnds 1–43 (1–47, 1–3, 1–7, 1–11, 1–15) once more—Sleeve measures approx 16¼ (16¾, 17¼, 17¾, 18¼, 18¾)". End last rnd 8 (9, 10, 11, 12, 13) sts before marker.

AT THE SAME TIME, when Sleeve measures 1¾" from beg, inc 2 sts each side of marker on next rnd, then every 10 rnds 5 (0, 0, 0, 0, 0) times, every 8 rnds 7 (14, 10, 6, 2, 0) times, and every 6 rnds 0 (0, 6, 12, 18, 22) times as follows: K1, M1, knit to last st, M1, k1—107 (115, 123, 131, 139, 147) sts.

Note: Cap shaping and color work pattern occur simultaneously; please read the following section all the way through before continuing.

Shape Cap: BO 17 (19, 21, 23, 25, 27) sts, knit to end—90 (96, 102, 108, 114, 120) sts.

Next rnd: Pm, CO 10 steek sts over armhole bind-off, pm, knit to end. Dec 1 st on each side of steek every rnd 8 (9, 10, 10, 11, 11) times, then every other rnd 12 (13, 14, 16, 17, 19) times, then every rnd 9 (10, 11, 11, 12, 12) times as follows: K1, k2tog, knit to last 3 sts, ssk, k1, work steek—32 (32, 32, 34, 34, 36) sts rem. BO all sts.

AT THE SAME TIME, when 1 (2, 2, 2, 2, 2) full (7-rnd) Peerie bands have been completed following the beg of cap, work Rnds 1–19 of Yoke Chart. Cont to work Peerie Chart, beg with the next band in sequence.

FINISHING

Cut center front and armhole steeks between 5th and 6th sts. Sew shoulder seams.

Band: With RS facing, using longer circ needle and A, pick up and knit 205 (210, 217, 222, 229, 234) sts along right Front edge inside steek sts, 60 (62, 64, 66, 68, 70) sts along back neckline, and 205 (210, 217, 222, 229, 234) sts along left Front edge inside steek sts—470 (482, 498, 510, 526, 538) sts. Work Rows 1–5 of Ribbing Chart.

Buttonhole row (RS): Working Row 6 of Ribbing Chart, work 1 (5, 9, 13, 17, 21) st(s), *ssk, yo with both strands, k2tog, work 12 sts in patt as est; rep from * 10 more times, work in patt to end.

Finish Ribbing Chart, knitting into front and back of yo's on row following buttonholes. BO all sts.

Cut sleeve cap steeks between 5th and 6th sts. Sew sleeves into armholes inside steek sts. Trim steeks and finish with an overcast stitch. Sew buttons opposite buttonholes. Weave in loose ends. Block to finished measurements.

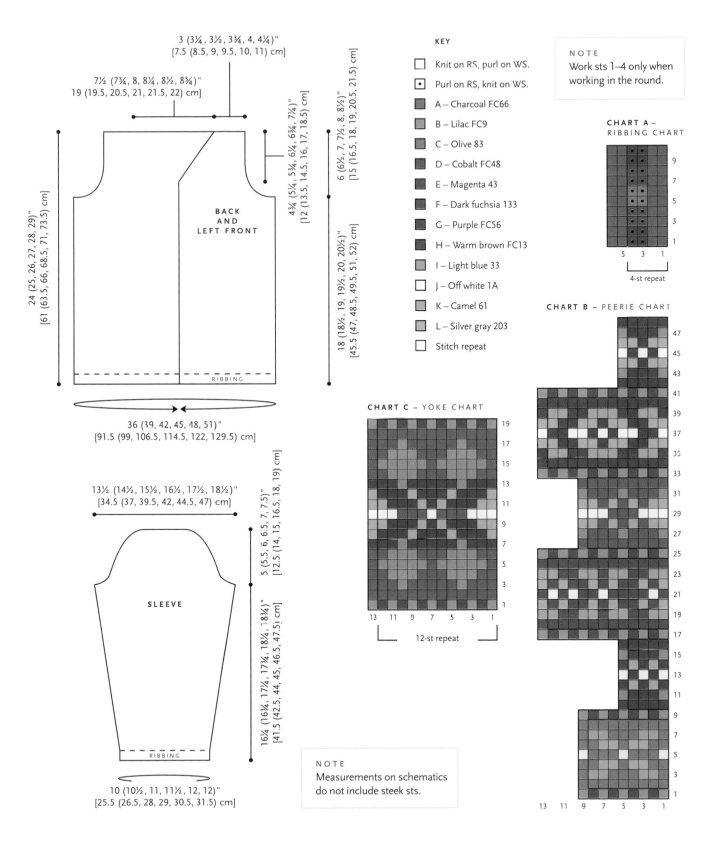

3 (3¼, 3½, 3¾, 4, 4¼)"
[7.5 (8.5, 9, 9.5, 10, 11) cm]

7½ (7¾, 8, 8¼, 8½, 8¾)"
19 (19.5, 20.5, 21, 21.5, 22) cm]

24 (25, 26, 27, 28, 29)"
[61 (63.5, 66, 68.5, 71, 73.5) cm]

BACK
AND
LEFT FRONT

RIBBING

4¾ (5¼, 5¾, 6¼, 6¾, 7¼)"
[12 (13.5, 14.5, 16, 17, 18.5) cm]

6 (6½, 7, 7½, 8, 8½)"
[15 (16.5, 18, 19, 20.5, 21.5) cm]

18 (18½, 19, 19½, 20, 20½)"
[45.5 (47, 48.5, 49.5, 51, 52) cm]

36 (39, 42, 45, 48, 51)"
[91.5 (99, 106.5, 114.5, 122, 129.5) cm]

13½ (14½, 15½, 16½, 17½, 18½)"
[34.5 (37, 39.5, 42, 44.5, 47) cm]

SLEEVE

RIBBING

5 (5.5, 6, 6.5, 7, 7.5)"
[12.5 (14, 15, 16.5, 18, 19) cm]

16¼ (16¾, 17¼, 17¾, 18¼, 18¾)"
[41.5 (42.5, 44, 45, 46.5, 47.5) cm]

10 (10½, 11, 11½, 12, 12)"
[25.5 (26.5, 28, 29, 30.5, 31.5) cm]

KEY

☐ Knit on RS, purl on WS.

⊡ Purl on RS, knit on WS.

▨ A – Charcoal FC66

▨ B – Lilac FC9

▨ C – Olive 83

▨ D – Cobalt FC48

▨ E – Magenta 43

▨ F – Dark fuchsia 133

▨ G – Purple FC56

▨ H – Warm brown FC13

▨ I – Light blue 33

☐ J – Off white 1A

▨ K – Camel 61

▨ L – Silver gray 203

☐ Stitch repeat

NOTE
Work sts 1–4 only when
working in the round.

CHART A –
RIBBING CHART

4-st repeat

CHART B – PEERIE CHART

CHART C – YOKE CHART

12-st repeat

NOTE
Measurements on schematics
do not include steek sts.

SKI JACKET

SIZES
X-Small (Small, Medium, Large,
X-Large) Shown in Small

FINISHED MEASUREMENTS
Chest: 33¾ (38¼, 44, 48½, 52¼)"
(closed)

YARN
Reynolds Lopi (100% wool;
110 yds / 100 g): 6 (7, 8, 10, 11) balls
#47 red (MC); 2 (2, 2, 3, 3) balls each
#9985 green (A) and #87 brown (B);
1 ball each #98 blue (C) and #364
off-white (D)

NEEDLES
One 32" circular (circ) needle size
US 10½ (6.5 mm)
One set of five double-pointed needles
(dpn) size US 10½ (6.5 mm)
Change needle size if necessary to
obtain correct gauge.

NOTIONS
Stitch markers, stitch holders, yarn
needle, five ¾" shank buttons

GAUGE
14 sts and 20 rows = 4" (10 cm) in
Stockinette st (St st)

STITCH PATTERN
Twisted Rib (multiple of 2 sts)
Row (or Rnd) 1: *K1-tbl, p1-tbl; rep
from *.
Row 2: *P1-tbl, k1-tbl, rep from *.
Rep Rows 1 and 2 for working back
and forth.
Rep Rnd 1 for working in the round.

NOTES
▸ This project is worked back and forth;
  a circular needle is required to accommodate the large number of sts.
▸ Work edge sts in St st.

In the 1950s, the Mary Maxim company made a big splash in Canada with brightly-colored sweaters based on the work of the Salish Indians from the Cowichan Reservation on Vancouver Island. The Cowichan began making sweaters before World War I; their trademark garment was a heavy, shawl-collared cardigan featuring graphed geometric, floral, and pictoral motifs in two-color stranded knitting and naturally colored yarns.

Mary Maxim sweaters, which featured similar pictoral motifs—horses, geese, bison, hockey players—knit in intarsia and heavy yarns, were so popular that almost everyone had one, or wished they did. They were even donned by the rich and famous, from visiting comedian Bob Hope to Princess Anne and the prime minister of Canada. Vintage Mary Maxim sweaters still show up periodically on eBay. My version sports a modified shawl collar and Cowichan geometric patterning worked in multiple colors and stranded knitting, but I have set the motif against a bright background color, atypical for both the Salish and Mary Maxim designs, to lighten up those chilly winter days.

BODY

Using A and circ needle, CO 111 (127, 147, 163, 177) sts.
Begin Twisted Rib: (RS) K1 (edge st), work Twisted Rib to last 2 sts, end k1-tbl, k1 (edge st). Change to MC. Maintaining edge sts in St st, work 6 more rows of Twisted Rib.
Lower Border: (WS) Change to St st and work even for 3 rows. Work Rnds 1–3 of Yoke Pattern for Border. Using MC, work 4 rows in St st.
Set Up for Waist Shaping: (WS) P11 (13, 15, 17, 19), pm for right front dart, p15 (17, 20, 22, 23), pm for right side seam, p16 (18, 21, 23, 25), pm for right back dart, p27 (31, 35, 39, 43), pm for left back dart, p16 (18, 21, 23, 25), pm for left side seam, p15 (17, 20, 22, 23), pm for left front dart, purl to end.

Decrease row: (RS) Knit to marker, slip marker (sm); [ssk, knit to 2 sts before next marker, k2tog, sm] twice; knit to next marker, sm; ssk, knit to 2 sts before next marker, k2tog, sm; ssk, knit to 2 sts before last marker, k2tog, sm; knit to end—8 sts dec'd. Work 3 rows even. Rep Dec row—95 (111, 131, 147, 161) sts rem. Work 3 rows even.
Increase row: (RS) Knit to first marker, sm; k1, M1-L, knit to 1 st before next marker, M1-R, k1, sm; k1, M1-L, knit to 1 st before next marker, M1-R, k1, sm; knit to next marker, sm; k1, M1-L, knit to 1 st before next marker, M1-R, k1, sm; k1, M1-L, knit to 1 st before last marker, M1-R, k1, sm, knit to end— 8 sts inc'd. Work 12 rows even. Rep Inc row—111 (127, 147, 163, 177) sts. Removing markers on first row, work even in St st until Body measures

11¾ (12, 12¼, 12½, 13)" from beg, ending with a RS row.

Divide for Fronts and Back: (WS) P21 (25, 29, 33, 35), p10 (10, 12, 12, 14) sts for left underarm and place on holder; p49 (57, 65, 73, 79) sts for Back, p10 (10, 12, 12, 14) sts for right underarm and place on holder; purl to end. Set aside, but do not break yarn.

SLEEVES (make 2)

Using dpns and A, CO 32 (34, 38, 40, 44) sts. Place marker (pm) for beg of rnd and join, being careful not to twist sts.

Begin Twisted Rib: (RS) Work 1 rnd of Twisted Rib. Change to MC, and work 8 more rnds of Twisted Rib.

Lower Border: (WS) Change to St st, and work 2 rnds, increasing 2 sts evenly on first rnd—34 (36, 40, 42, 46) sts. Work Rnds 1–3 of Chart, then work 6 rnds in St st with MC only.

Shape Sleeves: (RS) Inc 1 st at each side of marker on next rnd, then every 10 (10, 8, 8, 6) rnds 3 (4, 5, 6, 8) more times as follows: K1, M1-L, knit to last st, M1-R, k1—42 (46, 52, 56, 64) sts. Work even in St st until piece measures 15½ (16, 16½, 17, 17½)" from beg, ending 5 (5, 6, 6, 7) sts before marker.

Next Rnd: K10 (10, 12, 12, 14) sts for underarm and place on holder; knit to end of rnd—32 (36, 40, 44, 50) sts rem. Break yarn and set aside.

YOKE

Using yarn attached to Body, k21 (25, 29, 33, 35) right Front sts, pm for front seam; k32 (36, 40, 44, 50) Sleeve sts, pm for back seam; k49 (57, 65, 73, 79) Back sts, pm for back seam; k32 (36, 40, 44, 50) Sleeve sts; pm for left Front seam, knit to end—155 (179, 203, 227, 249) sts. Work even until yoke measures 3½ (3¾, 4, 4¼, 4¾)", ending with a WS row and decreasing 2 (2, 2, 2, 0) sts on last row—153 (177, 201, 225, 249) sts.

Establish Pattern: (RS) K1 (edge st), work 12-st rep of Chart 12 (14, 16, 18, 20) times, ending with 7 sts as indicated on chart, k1 (edge st). Cont patt as est, work Rows 2–21 of Chart, decreasing as indicated on Rows 7, 15, and 19—103 (119, 135, 151, 167) sts rem. Change to MC and purl 1 row.

Shape Neck: (RS) K1 (edge st), k1, *k2tog, k2; rep from * to last st, k1 (edge st)—78 (90, 102, 114, 126) sts rem. Work 3 rows even.

Next row: K1 (edge st), *k1, k2tog; rep from * to last 2 sts, k1, k1 (edge st)—53 (61, 69, 77, 85) sts rem. Purl 1 row.

Collar: Work 12 rows in Twisted Rib as for lower Body.

Front Borders: (RS) Cont in patt as est, work 53 (61, 69, 77, 85) collar sts; *do not turn*; with WS facing, pick up and knit 12 sts along side of collar (edge sts should be invisible from WS); then, with RS facing, pick up and knit 75 (77, 79, 81, 83) sts along left edge (edge sts should be invisible from RS).

Next row: Slip 1, [k1-tbl, p1-tbl] to top of collar, pm, p1, work 51 (55, 63, 71, 79) top collar sts in patt as est, pm, p1; *do not turn*; pick up and knit 12 sts along right collar edge as for left side, and 75 (77, 79, 81, 83) sts along right edge as for left—227 (239, 251, 263, 275) sts.

Shape Collar: (RS) Inc 2 sts at each side of top collar edge on this row, then every other row twice more as follows: Slip 1, [k1-tbl, p1-tbl] to marker, M1,

sm; k1, M1, work in patt to marker, M1, sm; k1, M1, work in patt as est to end of row—239 (251, 263, 275, 287) sts.
AT THE SAME TIME, on 2nd WS row, work Buttonhole row as follows:
Buttonhole row: (WS) Slip 1, p1-tbl, *k2tog-tbl, yo, k14 (16, 16, 16, 16); rep from * 4 times, k2tog-tbl, yo, work to end of row.
Work 3 rows. Change to A and work 1 row in patt as est. BO in patt.

FINISHING

Graft live sts of sleeves and body at underarms using Kitchener st (see Special Techniques, page 136). Sew on buttons opposite buttonholes. Weave in all ends. Block to finished measurements.

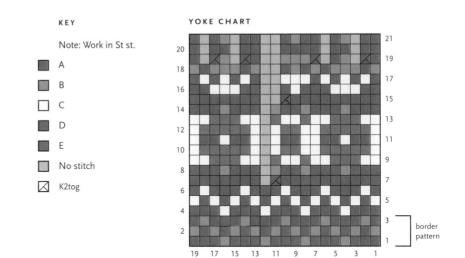

KEY

Note: Work in St st.

- ■ A
- ■ B
- □ C
- ■ D
- ■ E
- ■ No stitch
- ⌧ K2tog

YOKE CHART

border pattern

12-st repeat

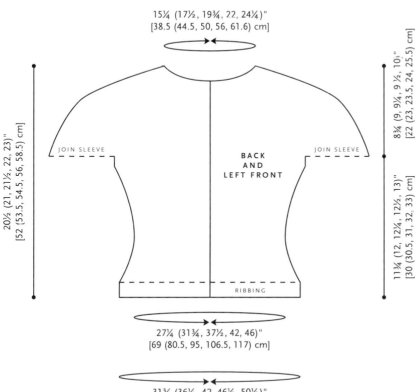

15¼ (17½, 19¾, 22, 24¼)"
[38.5 (44.5, 50, 56, 61.6) cm]

8¾ (9, 9¼, 9½, 10)"
[22 (23, 23.5, 24, 25.5) cm]

20½ (21, 21½, 22, 23)"
[52 (53.5, 54.5, 56, 58.5) cm]

JOIN SLEEVE   JOIN SLEEVE

BACK
AND
LEFT FRONT

RIBBING

11¾ (12, 12¼, 12½, 13)"
[30 (30.5, 31, 32, 33) cm]

27¼ (31¾, 37½, 42, 46)"
[69 (80.5, 95, 106.5, 117) cm]

31¾ (36¼, 42, 46½, 50½)"
[80.5 (92, 106.5, 118, 128.5) cm]

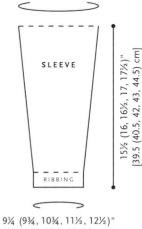

12 (13¼, 14¾, 16, 18¼)"
[30.5 (33.5, 37.5, 40.5, 46.5) cm]

SLEEVE

RIBBING

15½ (16, 16½, 17, 17½)"
[39.5 (40.5, 42, 43, 44.5) cm]

9¼ (9¾, 10¾, 11½, 12½)"
[23.5 (25, 27.5, 29, 32) cm]

LAYERED SKATER'S TOP

SIZES
X-Small (Small, Medium/Large,
X-Large, 2X-Large) Shown in size Small

FINISHED MEASUREMENTS
Chest: 31½ (36½, 41¼, 46, 50¾)"

YARN
Rowan Kid Silk Haze (70% kid
mohair / 30% silk; 227 yds / 25 g):
2 (2, 3, 3, 4) balls #596 marmalade

NEEDLES
One 24" circular (circ) needle size
US 4 (3.5 mm)
One 24" circular needle size
US 6 (4 mm)
One set of five double-pointed
needles (dpn) size US 6 (4 mm)
Change needle size if necessary to
obtain correct gauge.

NOTIONS
Waste yarn, yarn needle, stitch
markers (one in contrasting color for
beg of rnd), stitch holders, cable
needle (cn)

GAUGE
20 sts and 30 rows = 4" (10 cm) in
Fir Cone pattern (see Chart A) using
larger needle

The fashion of layering a short-sleeved T-shirt over a long-sleeved one dates from the 1970s, when competing skateboarders began wearing T-shirts supplied by different sponsors. The athletes wore these promotional tees over their own long-sleeved shirts, which were warmer and afforded better protection.

Based on designer Elizabeth Zimmermann's circular sweater designs, these two tops incorporate traditional elements—Shetland lace patterns and cables—and seamless construction. Worn together, they're a contrast of textures—one smooth and straightforward, the other soft and lacy, but still modern.

Overtop

BODY
Using smaller needle, CO 158 (182, 206, 230, 254) sts. Place marker (pm) for beg of rnd and join, being careful not to twist sts. [Purl 1 rnd, knit 1 rnd] three times. Change to larger needles.
Establish Pattern: Work Rnd 1 of Fir Cone Chart across first 43 (49, 55, 61, 67) sts, pm, work Row 1 of Tree Chart across next 17 sts, pm, k19 (25, 31, 37, 43), pm, work 79 (91, 103, 115, 127) Back sts in Fir Cone Chart.
Work patt as est until Body measures approx 10¼ (10¾, 11¼, 11¾, 12¼)" or desired length to underarms, ending ready to begin a non-patterned rnd. Knit 1 rnd, ending 6 (6, 6, 12, 12) sts before end of rnd.
Divide for Front and Back:
Work 12 (12, 12, 24, 24) sts in patt and slip to holder; work 79 (91, 103, 115, 127) sts in patt as est, then slip last 12 (12, 12, 24, 24) sts worked to second

holder; work in patt to end. Set aside, but do not break yarn.

SLEEVE BANDS (make 2)
Using dpns, CO 69 (69, 81, 93, 105) sts. Place marker (pm) for beg of rnd and join, being careful not to twist sts. Purl 1 rnd, knit 1 rnd, purl 1 rnd, ending last rnd 6 (6, 6, 12, 12) sts before marker.
Next Rnd: K12 (12, 12, 24, 24) sts for underarm, place sts on holder; knit to end of rnd—57 (57, 69, 69, 81) sts rem for sleeve band. Break yarn and set aside.

YOKE
Join Sleeves: Using yarn attached to Body, k57 (57, 69, 69, 81) left Sleeve sts, pm, k67 (79, 91, 91, 103) Front sts, pm, k57 (57, 69, 69, 81) right Sleeve sts, pm, k67 (79, 91, 91, 103) Back sts—248 (272, 320, 320, 368) sts total. Pm for beg of rnd. Maintaining patt as est on Body, and working Sleeve sts in Fir Cone patt (beg on same rnd as

being worked on Body), work even until Rnd 8 of Fir Cone chart has been completed.

Shape Armholes on Front and Back: Dec 1 st at each armhole edge of Front and Back 3 (6, 9, 6, 9) times over next 4 (8, 12, 8, 12) rnds, working Dec Chart Rnds 1–4 (1–8; 1–8, then 1–4; 1–8; 1–8, then 1–4) as follows: K57 (57, 69, 69, 81) Sleeve sts, slip marker (sm), work Dec Chart, cont in patt across Front, end by working Dec Chart, sm; k57 (57, 69, 69, 81) Sleeve sts, sm; work Dec Chart, work in patt across Back, end by working Dec Chart—61 (67, 73, 79, 85) sts rem each Back and Front.

Shape Sleeve Cap: Dec 1 st at each sleeve edge [6 times over the next 8 rnds] 4 (4, 5, 5, 6) times following Dec Chart as follows: Beg with Rnd 5 (1, 5, 1, 5) of Dec Chart, work Dec Chart across Sleeve, sm; work Front in patt, sm; work Dec Chart across Sleeve, sm; work Back in patt—9 sts rem each sleeve. Work 1 non-patterned rnd.

Shape Neck: Remove first 2 markers and beg working back and forth in rows. Beg on left side, shape neck by decreasing at left shoulder as follows:

Row 1 (RS): Slip 1 wyib, work 7 sts in patt as est, ssk (last st of Sleeve cap together with first st of Body), turn.

Row 2: Slip 1 wyif, p7, p2tog, turn.

Row 3: Slip 1 wyib, work 7 sts in patt, sssk, turn.

Row 4: Slip 1 wyif, p7, p3tog, turn.

Rep [Rows 1–4] twice more, then [Rows 1–3] once more.

Next row (WS): Slip 1 wyif, p7, p3tog, replace beg-of-rnd marker, purl across to next marker and remove it, p7, p3tog, turn. Cont decreasing at right shoulder

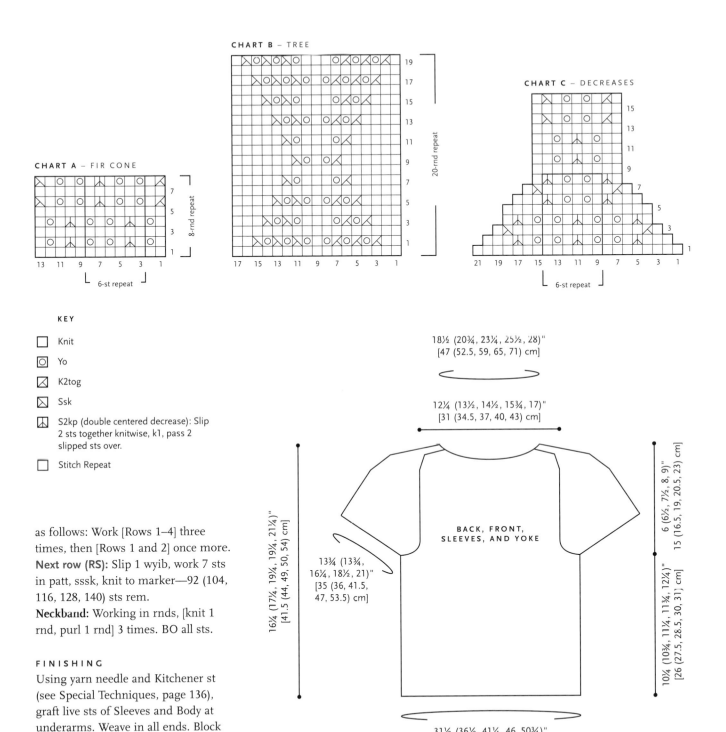

CHART B – TREE

20-rnd repeat

19
17
15
13
11
9
7
5
3
1

17 15 13 11 9 7 5 3 1

CHART C – DECREASES

15
13
11
9
7
5
3
1

21 19 17 15 13 11 9 7 5 3 1

⌐ 6-st repeat ¬

CHART A – FIR CONE

7
5
3
1

8-rnd repeat

13 11 9 7 5 3 1

⌐ 6-st repeat ¬

KEY

☐ Knit

◯ Yo

⧄ K2tog

⧅ Ssk

⧊ S2kp (double centered decrease): Slip
2 sts together knitwise, k1, pass 2
slipped sts over.

☐ Stitch Repeat

as follows: Work [Rows 1–4] three
times, then [Rows 1 and 2] once more.
Next row (RS): Slip 1 wyib, work 7 sts
in patt, sssk, knit to marker—92 (104,
116, 128, 140) sts rem.
Neckband: Working in rnds, [knit 1
rnd, purl 1 rnd] 3 times. BO all sts.

FINISHING
Using yarn needle and Kitchener st
(see Special Techniques, page 136),
graft live sts of Sleeves and Body at
underarms. Weave in all ends. Block
to finished measurements.

18½ (20¾, 23¼, 25½, 28)"
[47 (52.5, 59, 65, 71) cm]

12¼ (13½, 14½, 15¾, 17)"
[31 (34.5, 37, 40, 43) cm]

16¼ (17¼, 19¼, 19¾, 21¼)"
[41.5 (44, 49, 50, 54) cm]

13¾ (13¾,
16¼, 18½, 21)"
[35 (36, 41.5,
47, 53.5) cm]

**BACK, FRONT,
SLEEVES, AND YOKE**

6 (6½, 7½, 8, 9)"
15 (16.5, 19, 20.5, 23) cm]

10¼ (10¾, 11¼, 11¾, 12¼)"
[26 (27.5, 28.5, 30, 31) cm]

31½ (36½, 41¼, 46, 50¾)"
[80 (92.5, 105, 117, 129) cm]

Undertop

SIZES
Woman's X-Small (Small, Medium, Large, X-Large, 2X-Large)
Shown in size Small

FINISHED MEASUREMENTS
Chest: 33 (36½, 40, 43½, 47, 50½)"

YARN
Rowan Cotton Glace (100% cotton; 125 yds / 50 g): 8 (9, 10, 11, 12, 13) balls #808 mystic

NEEDLES
One 24" circular (circ) needle size US 2 (2.75 mm)
One 24" circular needle size US 3 (3.25 mm)
One set of five double-pointed needles (dpn) size US 2 (2.75 mm)
One set of five double-pointed needles size US 3 (3.25 mm)
Change needle size if necessary to obtain correct gauge.

NOTIONS
Stitch markers (one in contrasting color for beg of rnd), stitch holders, yarn needle, cable needle (cn)

GAUGE
23 sts and 33 rows = 4" (10 cm) in Stockinette st (St st) using larger needles

BODY

Hem: Using smaller circ needle, CO 186 (206, 226, 246, 266, 286) sts. Place marker (pm) for beg of rnd and join, being careful not to twist sts. Knit 7 rnds. Purl 1 rnd (turning rnd). Change to larger circ needle, and knit 3 (5, 7, 3, 5, 7) rnds.

Shape Waist: Pm for second side seam as follows: K93 (103, 113, 123, 133, 143), pm, knit to end. Dec 1 st on each side of markers on next rnd, then every 5 (5, 5, 6, 6, 6) rnds 5 more times as follows: *K1, ssk, knit to 3 sts before marker, k2tog, k1; rep from * once more—162 (182, 202, 222, 242, 262) sts. Knit 6 rnds. Inc 1 st on each side of markers on next rnd, then every 9 (9, 9, 10, 10, 10) rnds 6 more times as follows: *K1, M1-L, knit to 1 st before marker, M1-R, k1; rep from * once more—190 (210, 230, 250, 270, 290) sts. Work even in St st until piece measures 11¾ (12½, 12¾, 13¼, 13½, 14)" from turning rnd, ending last rnd 7 (8, 9, 10, 11, 12) sts before beg-of-rnd marker.

Divide for Front and Back: K14 (16, 18, 20, 22, 24) sts and slip to holder for underarm; k95 (105, 115, 125, 135, 145) and slip last 14 (16, 18, 20, 22, 24) sts worked to holder for underarm; knit to end—81 (89, 97, 105, 113, 121) sts each Front and Back. Set aside, but do not break yarn.

SLEEVES (make 2)

Hem: Using smaller dpns, CO 42 (44, 48, 50, 54, 56) sts and distribute on four needles. Pm for beg of rnd and join, being careful not to twist sts. Knit 7 rnds. Purl 1 rnd (turning rnd). Change to larger dpns.

Establish Cable Pattern: K17 (18, 20, 21, 23, 24), p1, k1, M1, k4, M1, k1, p1, k17 (18, 20, 21, 23, 24)—44 (46, 50, 52, 56, 58) sts.

Next rnd: K17 (18, 20, 21, 23, 24), p1, work Rnd 1 of Cable (see Chart) over next 8 sts, p1, knit to end. Work even in patt as est for 9 (8, 7, 7, 5, 5) rnds.

Shape Sleeve: Inc 1 st on each side of marker on next rnd, then every 11 (10, 9, 9, 9, 8) rnds 10 (11, 12, 13, 14, 16) times as follows: K1, M1-L, work in patt as est to last st, M1-R, k1—66 (70, 76, 80, 86, 92) sts.
Work even until Sleeve measures 14¾ (15¼, 15½, 16, 16¼, 16¾)" from turning rnd, ending 7 (8, 9, 10, 11, 12) sts before marker.

Next Rnd: K14 (16, 18, 20, 22, 24) sts and place on holder for underarm; knit to end of rnd—52 (54, 58, 60, 64, 68) sts rem. Break yarn and set aside.

YOKE

Using yarn attached to Body, work left Sleeve sts in patt as est, pm, knit Front sts, pm, work right Sleeve sts in patt as est, pm, knit Back sts—266 (286, 310, 330, 354, 378) sts. Pm for beg of rnd. Maintaining patt as est on sleeves, work 5 rnds even.

Shape Armholes on Front and Back: Dec 1 st at each armhole edge of Front and Back on next 4 (5, 7, 8, 10, 11) rnds as follows: *Work in patt to marker, sm, k1, k2tog, knit to 3 sts before marker, ssk, k1, sm; rep from * once more—73 (79, 83, 89, 93, 99) sts rem on Front and Back. Work 1 rnd even.

Shape Sleeve Cap: Dec 1 st at each Sleeve edge on next rnd, then every other rnd 11 (11, 9, 9, 5, 5) times, then every rnd 7 (8, 12, 13, 19, 20) times as follows: K1, k2tog, work left Sleeve sts to 3 sts before marker, ssk, k1, sm; knit Front sts, sm; k1, k2tog, work right Sleeve sts to last 3 sts before marker, ssk, k1, sm, knit Back sts—14 sts rem each Sleeve.

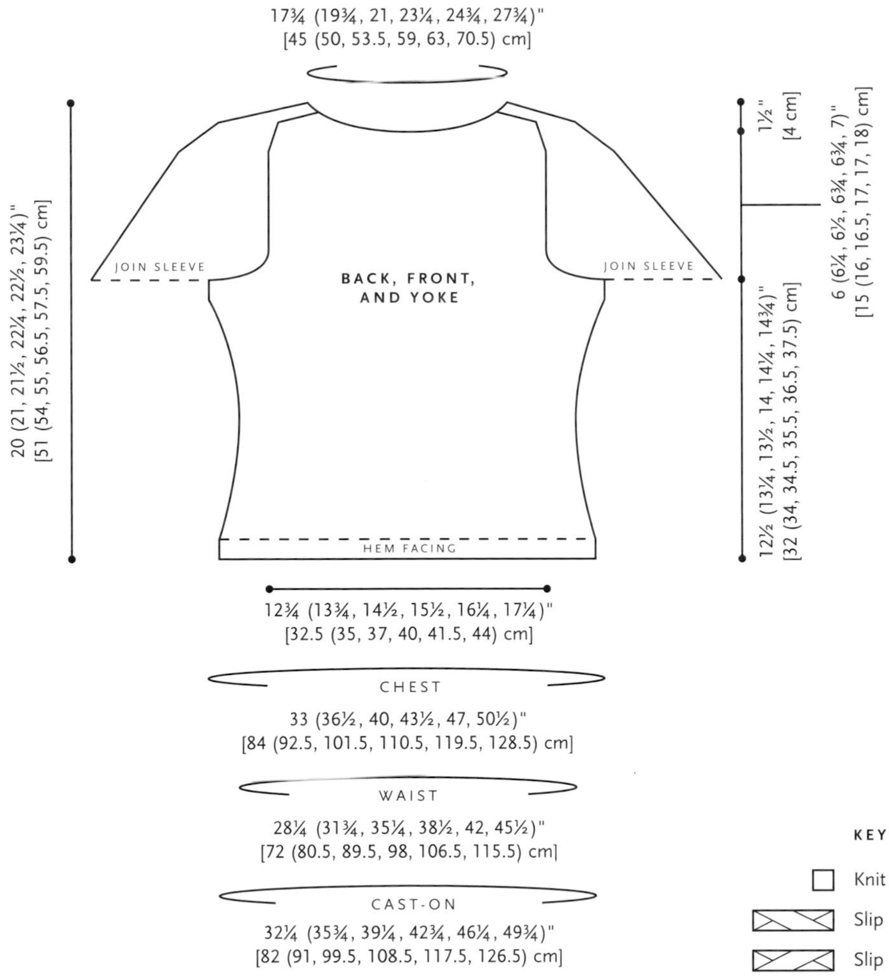
17¾ (19¾, 21, 23¼, 24¾, 27¾)"
[45 (50, 53.5, 59, 63, 70.5) cm]
20 (21, 21½, 22¼, 22½, 23¼)"
[51 (54, 55, 56.5, 57.5, 59.5) cm]
JOIN SLEEVE
BACK, FRONT, AND YOKE
JOIN SLEEVE
1½"
[4 cm]
6 (6¼, 6½, 6¾, 6¾, 7)"
[15 (16, 16.5, 17, 17, 18) cm]
12½ (13¼, 13½, 14, 14¼, 14¾)"
[32 (34, 34.5, 35.5, 36.5, 37.5) cm]
HEM FACING
12¾ (13¾, 14½, 15½, 16¼, 17¼)"
[32.5 (35, 37, 40, 41.5, 44) cm]
CHEST
33 (36½, 40, 43½, 47, 50½)"
[84 (92.5, 101.5, 110.5, 119.5, 128.5) cm]
WAIST
28¼ (31¾, 35¼, 38½, 42, 45½)"
[72 (80.5, 89.5, 98, 106.5, 115.5) cm]
CAST-ON
32¼ (35¾, 39¼, 42¾, 46¼, 49¾)"
[82 (91, 99.5, 108.5, 117.5, 126.5) cm]

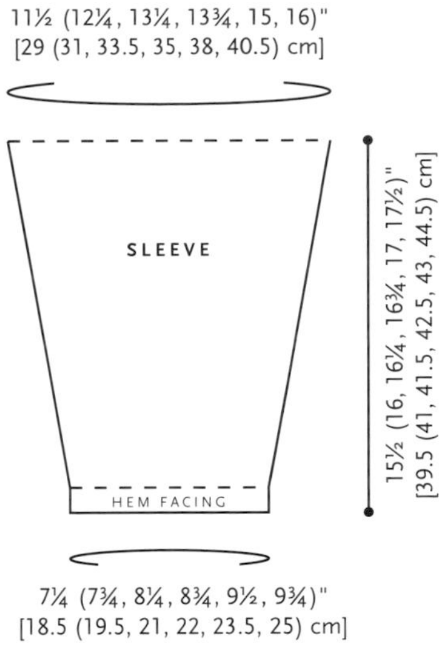
11½ (12¼, 13¼, 13¾, 15, 16)"
[29 (31, 33.5, 35, 38, 40.5) cm]
SLEEVE
15½ (16, 16¼, 16¾, 17, 17½)"
[39.5 (41, 41.5, 42.5, 43, 44.5) cm]
HEM FACING
7¼ (7¾, 8¼, 8¾, 9½, 9¾)"
[18.5 (19.5, 21, 22, 23.5, 25) cm]

CABLE CHART

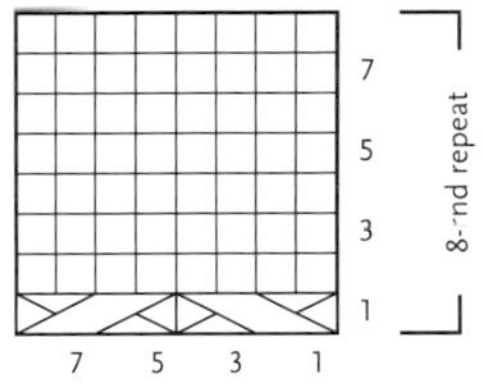
7
5
3
1
8-rnd repeat
7
5
3
1

KEY

- Knit on RS, purl on WS.
- Slip next 2 sts to cn, hold to front, k2, k2 from cn.
- Slip next 2 sts to cn, hold to back, k2, k2, from cn.

Shape Saddle Shoulders: *Work Sleeve sts in patt to 1 st before marker, slip next st, remove marker, replace slipped st on LH needle, then replace marker on RH needle (marker shifted 1 st to right); ssk, knit to 1 st before next marker, slip 1 st, remove marker, replace slipped st on LH needle, k2tog, replace marker (marker shifted 1 st to left); rep from * once more—4 sts decreased (2 each Front and Back). Cont to dec 1 st at each shoulder edge of Front and Back on next 9 rnds as follows: *Work 12 sts in patt, sm, ssk, knit to 2 sts before next marker, k2tog; rep from * once more—53 (59, 63, 69, 73, 79) sts rem Front and Back and 12 sts on each saddle.

Shape Neck: Removing first 2 markers, beg working back and forth in rows as follows:

Row 1 (RS): Slip 1 wyib, work 10 sts in patt, ssk (last st of saddle and first st of Body), turn.

Row 2: Slip 1 wyif, work 10 sts in patt, p2tog (last st of saddle and first st of Body), turn.

Rep [Rows 1 and 2] 6 more times, then work Row 1 once more.

Next row (WS): Slip 1 wyif, work 10 sts in patt, p2tog; replace beg-of-rnd marker, then purl to next marker and remove it; work 11 sts in patt, slip 1 st, remove marker, replace slipped st on LH needle, p2tog, turn. Rep [Rows 1 and 2] 6 times.

Next row: Slip 1 wyib, work 10 sts in patt, ssk, knit to beg-of-rnd marker.

Neckband: Knit 6 rnds. BO all sts very loosely.

FINISHING

Using yarn needle and Kitchener st (see SpecialTechniques, page 136), graft underarm sts of Sleeves and Body. Fold Sleeve and Body hems to WS and sew into place. Weave in all ends. Block to finished measurements.

GRAPHIC HOODIE

SIZES
X-Small (Small, Medium, Large,
X-Large, 2X-Large)
Shown in size Small

FINISHED MEASUREMENTS
Chest: 33¾ (37¼, 40¾, 44½, 48, 51½)"

YARN
Dale of Norway Heilo (100% wool;
109yds / 50 g): 12 (12, 14, 14, 16, 17)
balls #90 black (MC); 3 (3, 4, 4, 4, 5) balls
#0017 white (A); 1 ball #4137 red (B).

NEEDLES
One 32" circular (circ) needle size
US 4 (3.5 mm)
One 32" circular needle size
US 5 (3.75 mm)
One set of five double-pointed needles
(dpn) size US 4 (3.5 mm)
One set of five double-pointed needles
size US 5 (3.75 mm)
Change needle size if necessary to obtain
correct gauge.

NOTIONS
Stitch markers, stitch holders, yarn
needle

GAUGE
27 sts and 31 rnds = 4" (10 cm) in
stranded Stockinette st (St st) using
larger needles

STITCH PATTERN
Checkerboard Rib (multiple of 4 sts)
Rnds 1–3, 7–9: [K2, p2] around.
Rnds 4–6: [P2, k2] around.

NOTE
▶ To avoid color jog on sleeve, always
work first and last sts in round with MC.

This hoodie is based on the Setesdal sweaters that have been part of the folk costume in southern Norway since the mid-19th century. Setesdal sweaters are knit mainly in black and white with a small allover pattern—hence the local name "spotted" or "lice" sweaters. These garments often feature different, harmonious motifs set off by double lines at the yoke, upper sleeves, and cuffs, as well as red embroidery at the cuffs and neckband.

Departing from the traditional technique, I knit this sweater in the round only to the underarms, then added set-in sleeves for a good fit. You can easily obtain the look of the traditional Setesdal sweater, however, by knitting a tube without any shaping and cutting down the armholes with sewing shears, as the Norwegians do.

BODY
Work Checkerboard Rib Pattern: Using smaller circ needle and MC, CO 228 (252, 276, 300, 324, 348) sts. Place marker (pm) for beg of rnd and join, being careful not to twist sts. Work 9 rnds of Checkerboard Rib. Change to larger circ needles and knit 6 rnds.
Establish Color Patterns: Work Rnds 3–9 of Narrow Border Chart once. Work Rnds 1–4 of Lice Pattern Chart until Body measures 14¼ (14½, 14¾, 15, 15¼, 15½)", ending 4 (5, 6, 3, 4, 4) sts before marker on last rnd.
Divide for Front and Back: Maintaining Lice patt, BO 8 (10, 12, 6, 8, 8) sts for underarm, k106 (116, 126, 144, 154, 166) sts and put on holder for Front, BO 8 (10, 12, 6, 8, 8) sts for underarm, knit to end.

BACK
[Larger 3 sizes only]: (WS) Working back and forth in Lice Pattern on Back sts only, BO - (-, -, 4, 4, 5) sts at beg of next 2 rows—106 (116, 126, 136, 146, 156) sts rem.

[All sizes]: (WS) Work 1 row even in patt.
Shape Armholes and Begin Border Pattern: (RS) Dec 1 st at each edge of every RS row 10 (12, 14, 16, 18, 20) times as follows: K2, ssk, knit to last 4 sts, k2tog, k2—86 (92, 98, 104, 110, 116) sts rem. AT THE SAME TIME, when armholes measure 1 (1¼, 1½, 1¾, 2, 2¼)" *and* Row 2 OR 4 of Lice Pattern has been completed, work Rows 1–47 of Wide Border Chart, taking care to center pattern (See Special Techniques, page 136).
Shape Shoulders and Back Neck: (WS) With MC, p27 (28, 30, 31, 32, 34), pm, p32 (36, 38, 42, 46, 48), pm, purl to end.
Row 1: BO 4 (4, 5, 5, 5, 6) sts, knit to 4 sts before first marker, ssk, k2, remove marker, join in a second ball of yarn, knit to next marker and place these last 32 (36, 38, 42, 46, 48) sts on holder for Back neck, remove second marker, k2, k2tog, knit to end.
Row 2: (left shoulder) BO 4 (4, 5, 5, 5, 6) sts, knit to last 4 sts of left side, p2tog, p2; (right shoulder) p2, ssp, purl to end. Cont work on both sides at the same

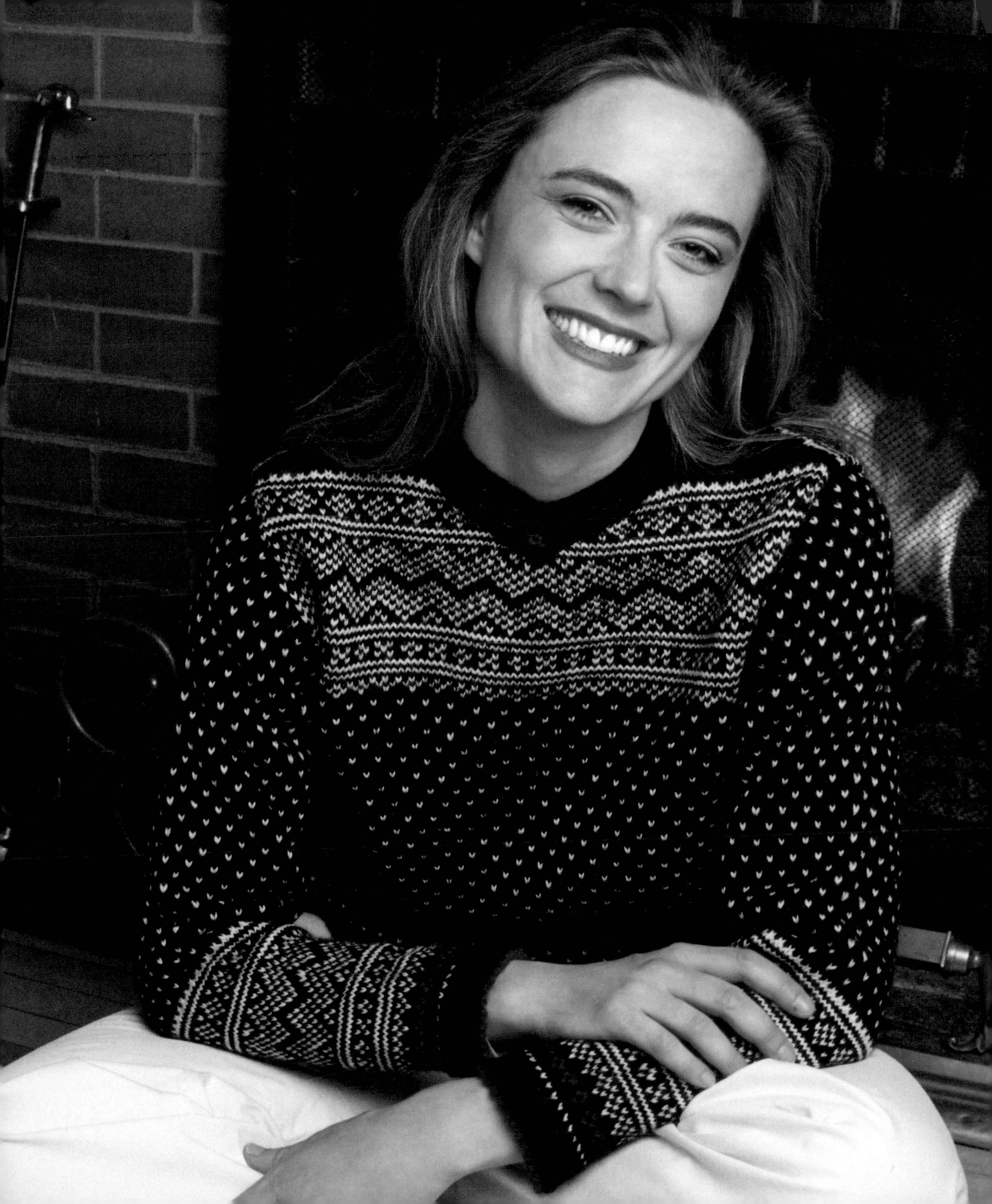

time, dec 1 st at each neck edge every RS row 3 more times and BO 4 sts at each shoulder edge 1 (0, 0, 0, 0, 0) time(s), 5 sts 3 (4, 3, 2, 1, 0) time(s), and 6 sts 0 (0, 1, 2, 3, 4) time(s).

FRONT

Work as for Back until armholes measure 5", ending with a WS row.
Shape Right Neck: (RS) K43 (46, 49, 52, 55, 58) sts and place on holder for left Front, knit to end. Working on right neck only, dec 1 st at neck edge every row 20 (22, 23, 25, 27, 28) times. AT THE SAME TIME, when Wide Border Chart has been completed, BO 4 sts at shoulder edge 2 (1, 0, 0, 0, 0) time(s), 5 sts 3 (4, 4, 3, 2, 0) times, and 6 sts 0 (0, 1, 2, 3, 5) time(s).
Shape Left Neck: (RS) Replace held neck sts. Shape as for right neck.

SLEEVES (make 2)

Hem Facing: With smaller dpns and B, CO 50 (53, 56, 59, 62, 65) sts. Distribute evenly on needles; pm for beg of rnd and join, being careful not to twist sts. Knit 8 rnds. Inc 8 (7, 8, 7, 8, 7) sts evenly on next rnd—58 (60, 64, 66, 70, 72) sts. Knit 1 rnd.
Picot Turning Round: *Yo, k2tog; rep from * around. Change to larger dpns and MC.
Next rnd: *K1, k1-tbl; rep from * to end. Knit 7 rnds, inc 1 st on 6th rnd—59 (61, 65, 67, 71, 73) sts.
Establish Color Patterns and Shape Sleeve: Work Rnds 1–9 of Narrow Border Chart (see Note). With MC, knit 1 rnd. Work Rnds 1–47 of Wide Border Chart. Work remainder of Sleeve in Lice Pattern.
AT THE SAME TIME, inc 2 sts on first Narrow Border rnd, then every 8 rnds 8 (4, 3, 0, 0, 0) times, every 6 rnds 6 (12, 14, 19, 18, 16) times, and every 4 rnds 0 (0, 0, 0, 2, 6) times as follows: K1MC, M1-L, work to 1 st before marker, M1-R, k1MC, working new sts in patt—89 (95, 101, 107, 113, 119) sts. Work even until Sleeve measures 16½ (17, 17½, 18, 18¼, 18¾)" from picot rnd, ending 4 (5, 6, 3, 4, 4) sts before marker on last rnd. BO 8 (10, 12, 6, 8, 8) sts, knit to end—81 (85, 89, 101, 105, 111) sts rem. Work back and forth in rows for remainder of sleeve.
[Larger 3 sizes only]: BO - (-, -, 4, 4, 5) sts at beg of next 2 rows.]
[All sizes]:
Shape Cap: (WS) Dec 1 st at each edge on next row, then every row 7 (8, 9, 9, 10, 11) times, then every other row 6 times, and then every row 12 (13, 14, 14, 15, 16) times, working WS and RS rows as follows: (WS) P2, p2tog, purl to last 4 sts, ssp, p2; (RS) K2, ssk, knit to last 4 sts, k2tog, k2—29 (29, 29, 33, 33, 33) sts rem. BO all sts.

HOOD

Sew shoulder seams.
With smaller circ needle and MC, with RS facing and beg at right shoulder, pick up and knit 9 (8, 8, 8, 8, 8) sts, knit up 32 (36, 38, 42, 46, 48) sts from Back neck holder, pick up and knit 9 (8, 8, 8, 8, 8) sts to left shoulder—50 (52, 54, 58, 62, 64) sts around Back neck. Knit 1 WS row. Work 5 rows in St st.
Next row: P21 (22, 23, 25, 27, 28), pm, p8, pm, purl to end.
Shape Back of Hood: (RS) Inc 1 st outside markers on next row, then every 4 rows 13 more times as follows: Knit to marker, M1-R, sm, k8, sm, M1-L, knit to end—78 (80, 82, 86, 90, 92) sts. Remove markers. Work even until Hood measures 10", ending with a RS row.
Next row: P36 (37, 38, 40, 42, 43), pm, k6, pm, knit to end. Dec 1 st outside markers on next row, then every other row 12 more times as follows: Knit to 2 sts before marker, k2tog, sm, k6, sm, ssk, knit to end—52 (54, 56, 60, 64, 66) sts. Purl 1 row.
Shape Top of Hood:
Row 1 (RS): Knit to second marker, sm, ssk, turn.
Row 2: Slip 1, sm, purl to marker, sm, ssp, turn.
Row 3: Slip 1, sm, knit to marker, sm, ssk, turn.
Rep Rows 2 and 3 until 8 sts rem. Place on holder. Cut yarn.
Hood and Neck Edging: (RS) Using smaller circ needles and MC, beg at center right Front neck, pick up and knit 26 (28, 29, 31, 33, 34) sts along right neck, 67 sts along Hood's right edge, 8 sts from holder, 67 sts along Hood's left edge, 26 (28, 29, 31, 33, 34) sts along left neck—194 (198, 200, 204, 208, 210) sts. *Do not join.* Knit 1 WS row. Work 2 rows in St st.
Border: (RS) Work Rows 3–5 of Narrow Border Chart. With MC, work 2 rows in St st. Work Rows 1–6 of Checkerboard Rib. BO all sts.

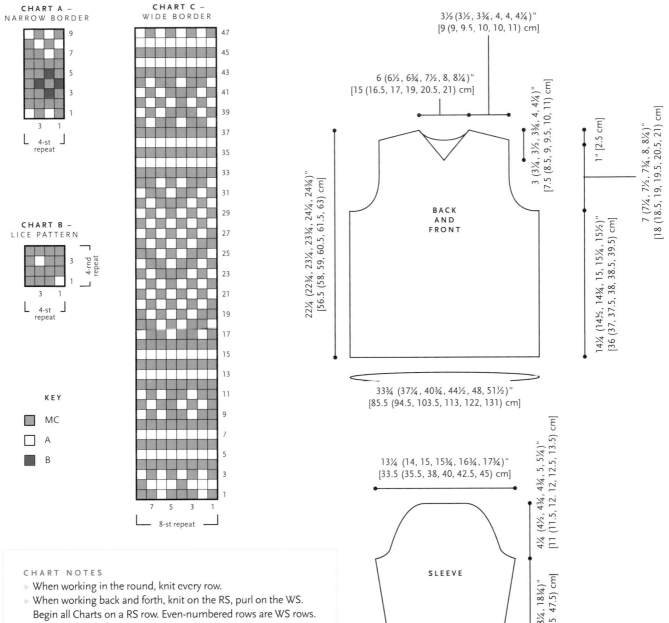

CHART A –
NARROW BORDER

9
7
5
3
1

3   1

⌞ 4-st ⌟
repeat

CHART C –
WIDE BORDER

47
45
43
41
39
37
35
33
31
29
27
25
23
21
19
17
15
13
11
9
7
5
3
1

7   5   3   1

⌞ 8-st repeat ⌟

CHART B –
LICE PATTERN

3
1

4-rnd
repeat

3   1

⌞ 4-st ⌟
repeat

KEY

☐ MC

☐ A

☐ B

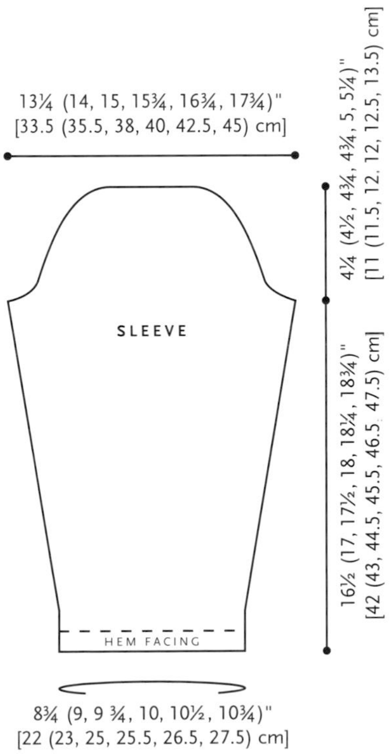

CHART NOTES

▸ When working in the round, knit every row.
▸ When working back and forth, knit on the RS, purl on the WS. Begin all Charts on a RS row. Even-numbered rows are WS rows.

FINISHING

Sew hood border's selvedges to neckline. Turn sleeve facings to WS and slipstitch into place. Sew sleeves into armholes. Weave in loose ends. Block to finished measurements.

3½ (3½, 3¾, 4, 4, 4¼)"
[9 (9, 9.5, 10, 10, 11) cm]

6 (6½, 6¾, 7½, 8, 8¼)"
[15 (16.5, 17, 19, 20.5, 21) cm]

3 (3¼, 3½, 3¾, 4, 4¼)"
[7.5 (8.5, 9, 9.5, 10, 11) cm]

1" [2.5 cm]

7 (7¼, 7½, 7¾, 8, 8¼)"
[18 (18.5, 19, 19.5, 20.5, 21) cm]

BACK AND FRONT

22¼ (22¾, 23¼, 23¾, 24¼, 24¾)"
[56.5 (58, 59, 60.5, 61.5, 63) cm]

14¼ (14½, 14¾, 15, 15¼, 15½)"
[36 (37, 37.5, 38, 38.5, 39.5) cm]

33¾ (37¼, 40¾, 44½, 48, 51½)"
[85.5 (94.5, 103.5, 113, 122, 131) cm]

13¼ (14, 15, 15¾, 16¾, 17¾)"
[33.5 (35.5, 38, 40, 42.5, 45) cm]

4¼ (4½, 4¾, 4¾, 5, 5¼)"
[11 (11.5, 12, 12, 12.5, 13.5) cm]

SLEEVE

16½ (17, 17½, 18, 18¼, 18¾)"
[42 (43, 44.5, 45.5, 46.5, 47.5) cm]

HEM FACING

8¾ (9, 9¾, 10, 10½, 10¾)"
[22 (23, 25, 25.5, 26.5, 27.5) cm]

ZIPPED VEST

SIZES
Men's Small (Medium, Large, X-Large, 2X-Large) Shown in size Large

FINISHED MEASUREMENTS
Chest: 38 (42, 45¾, 49½, 53¼)"

YARN
Patons Classic Wool (100% wool; 223 yds / 50 g): 5(5, 5, 6, 7) balls #225 dark grey mix

NEEDLE
One 32" circular (circ) needle size US 5 (3.75 mm)
Change needle size if necessary to obtain correct gauge.

NOTIONS
Stitch markers, stitch holders, yarn needle, sewing needle and thread in a matching color, 30" separating zipper

GAUGE
21 sts and 36 rows = 4" (10 cm) in Moss Stitch

STITCH PATTERNS
Moss Stitch (multiple of 2 sts; 4-row rep)
Rows 1 (WS) and 4: *K1, p1; rep from *.
Rows 2 and 3: *P1, k1; rep from *.
Rep Rows 1–4 for Moss Stitch.

Welt Pattern
Rows 1 (WS) and 2: Purl.
Rows 3 and 4: Knit.
Rep Rows 1–4 for Welt Pattern.

NOTES
▸ Although this project is worked back and forth, a circular needle is required to accommodate the large number of stitches.
▸ The zipper should be longer than the finished center opening and sewn from the bottom up; trim excess at the top and fold at a 45-degree angle. The collar facing will cover the raw edge.

Fishermen's sweaters are among the most popular sweaters in the world, and I am particularly fond of ganseys, the traditional sweaters worn broadly throughout the British Isles from as early as the mid-19th century. Named after the Channel Island of Guernsey where many originated, ganseys were traditionally knit in the round with dark blue or gray wool, using knit and purl stitches to form damask patterns, often of great beauty. They started out as warm, close-fitting undergarments, but the work of the fishermen's wives who mostly knit them was often so striking that, over a period of years, men began to wear them as outer garments, even on formal occasions.

The gansey's subtle, masculine patterning is distinctive yet adaptable to a variety of garment shapes. I have knit it up here as a warm, handsome, and practical zippered vest with a double-layer collar.

BODY
Using long tail method (see Special Techniques, page 136), CO 200 (220, 240, 260, 280) sts. Beg with a RS row, work 6 rows of Garter st.
Next Row (WS): K3, purl to last 3 sts, k3.
Next row: K3, place marker (pm), k42 (46, 50, 54, 58), pm, k10 (12, 14, 16, 18), pm, k90 (98, 106, 114, 122), pm, p10 (12, 14, 16, 18), pm, k42 (46, 50, 54, 58), pm, k3.
Establish Patterns:
Row 1 (WS): K3, sm, work Row 1 of Moss st to next marker, sm, *work Row 1 of Welt patt to next marker, sm, work Moss st to next marker, sm; rep from * to last 3 sts, k3.
Work 19 more rows in patts as est, maintaining 3-st Garter borders, Front and Back Moss st, and side panel Welts.
Body Welts: (WS)
Next 8 rows: Maintaining 3-st Garter borders, work Welt patt across Body. Work even in patt as est, alternating 20 rows of Moss st and 8 rows of Welt patt

on Fronts and Back until Body measures 13½ (14, 14¼, 14¾, 15)", ending with a WS row.
Establish Armhole Borders: (RS)
Next 6 rows: *Work in patt as est to 3 sts before side panel marker, k3, sm, knit to next marker, sm, k3; rep from * once more, work in patt to end of row.
Divide for Fronts and Back: (RS) Work in patt to second marker and place sts on holder for right Front; BO 10 (12, 14, 16, 18) sts; remove marker; work in patt to next marker and place sts on holder for Back; BO next 10 (12, 14, 16, 18) sts; work in patt to end—45 (49, 53, 57, 61) sts for each Front and 90 (98, 106, 114, 122) sts for Back.

LEFT FRONT
Row 1 (WS): K3, work in patt to last 3 sts, k3.
Shape Armhole: (RS) Maintaining 3-st Garter borders, dec 1 st at armhole edge on next row, and every other row 0 (0, 2, 5, 8) times, then every 4 rows 5

(6, 6, 5, 4) times as follows: K2, ssk, work in patt as est to last 3 sts, k3—39 (42, 44, 46, 48) sts rem. Work even in patt as est until armhole measures 5½ (5¾, 6, 6½, 6¾)", ending with a RS row.

Shape Neck: (WS) BO 5 (7, 7, 7, 8) sts at neck edge once, then BO 3 (3, 3, 4, 4) sts at beg of following 2 WS rows—28 (29, 31, 31, 32) sts rem. Work 1 RS row.

Begin Shoulder Welt Pattern: (WS) Maintaining 3-st Garter armhole border, work 13 rows of Welt patt, and AT THE SAME TIME, dec 1 st at neck edge on next row, then every other row 6 more times as follows: Work Welt patt to last 3 sts, ssk, k1—21 (22, 23, 24, 25) sts rem. Cut yarn, leaving an 8" tail. Place all sts on holder.

BACK

With WS facing, rejoin yarn; k3, work in patt as est to last 3 sts, k3.

Shape Armholes: (RS) Maintaining 3-st Garter borders, dec 1 st at each armhole edge on next row, then every other row 0 (0, 2, 5, 8) times, and every 4 rows 5 (6, 6, 5, 4) times as follows: K2, ssk, work in patt as est to last 4 sts, k2tog, k2—78 (84, 88, 92, 96) sts rem. Work even in patt until armholes measure 6 (6¼, 6½, 7, 7¼)", ending with a RS row.

Begin Shoulder Welt Pattern: (WS) Maintaining 3-st Garter borders, work 13 rows of Welt patt. Cut yarn, leaving a 32" tail. Place all sts on holder.

RIGHT FRONT

With WS facing, rejoin yarn; k3, work in patt as est to last 3 sts, k3.

Shape Armhole: (RS) Maintaining 3-st Garter borders, dec 1 st at each armhole edge on next row, then every other row 0 (0, 2, 5, 8) times, and every 4 rows 5 (6, 6, 5, 4) times as follows: K3, work in patt as est to last 4 sts, k2tog, k2—39 (42, 44, 46, 48) sts rem. Work even in patt as est until armhole measures 5½ (5¾, 6, 6½, 6¾)", ending with a WS row, having worked 1 more row than on left Front to neck shaping.

Shape Neck: (RS) BO 5 (7, 7, 7, 8) sts at neck edge once, then BO 3 (3, 3, 4, 4) sts at beg of following 2 RS rows—28 (29, 31, 31, 32) sts rem.

Begin Shoulder Welt Pattern: (WS) Maintaining 3-st Garter armhole border, work 13 rows of Welt patt, and AT THE SAME TIME, dec 1 st at neck edge on next row, then every other row 6 more times as follows: K1, k2tog, work Welt patt to last 3 sts, k3—21 (22, 23, 24, 25) sts rem. Cut yarn, leaving a 32" tail. Place all sts on holder.

FINISHING

With WS facing, working from the shoulder edges to neck and using tails, join Fronts to Back using 3-needle BO method (see Special Techniques, page 136).

COLLAR

(RS) Pick up and knit 24 (26, 27, 28, 29) left Front sts, 36 (40, 42, 44, 46) Back neck sts, 24 (26, 27, 28, 29) right Front sts—84 (92, 96, 100, 104) sts. Knit 1 row. Maintaining 3-st Garter borders, work 19 rows of Moss st (beg with Row 2), then 8 rows of Welt patt (beg with Row 3).

Make Facing: Maintaining 3-st Garter borders, work 3" in St st. BO all sts.

With matching sewing thread, sew in zipper (see Notes). Turn down facing of collar to WS, and sew into place using a yarn needle and knitting yarn. Weave in loose ends. Steam lightly.

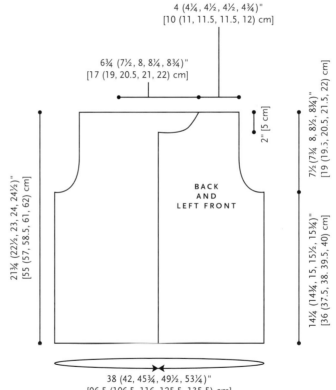

4 (4¼, 4½, 4½, 4¾)"
[10 (11, 11.5, 11.5, 12) cm]

6¾ (7½, 8, 8¼, 8¾)"
[17 (19, 20.5, 21, 22) cm]

2" [5 cm]

7½ (7¾, 8, 8½, 8¾)"
[19 (19.5, 20.5, 21.5, 22) cm]

BACK
AND
LEFT FRONT

21¾ (22½, 23, 24, 24½)"
[55 (57, 58.5, 61, 62) cm]

14¼ (14¾, 15, 15½, 15¾)"
[36 (37.5, 38, 39.5, 40) cm]

38 (42, 45¾, 49½, 53¼)"
[96.5 (106.5, 116, 125.5, 135.5) cm]

Montreal Tuque

SIZES
Small (Medium, Large)
To fit Child (Woman, Man)
Shown in size Large

FINISHED MEASUREMENTS
Circumference: 18 (20, 22)"

YARN
Plymouth Royal Cashmere (100% fine Italian cashmere; 154 yds / 50 g): 1 ball each #8511 navy (A), #8582 red (B), and #8072 off-white (C).
Note: Solid-colored or 2-color striped hat can be made from two balls.

NEEDLES
Set of five double-pointed needles (dpn) size US 4 (3.5 mm)
Change needle size if necessary to obtain correct gauge.

NOTIONS
Stitch marker, yarn needle

GAUGE
24 sts and 36 rows = 4" (10 cm) in 3x1 Rib

STITCH PATTERNS
3x1 Rib (multiple of 4 sts)
Pattern rnd: *K3, p1; rep from * around.

Stripe Sequence
5 rnds A, 2 rnds B, 1 rnd C, 2 rnds B.
Rep these 10 rnds for Stripe Sequence.

NOTE
▸ Do not break yarn between stripes. Carry unused yarn up wrong side.

Jacques Plante (a.k.a. Jake the Snake), one of the best goaltenders the world of hockey has known, backstopped the Montreal Canadiens to the Stanley Cup championship five consecutive times during the late 1950s. While his teammates played cards between events, Plante knit hats; he was especially renowned for his closely fitting ski bonnets, known in Québec as *tuques*. My version is knit in three colors of cashmere yarn in a warm and snug-fitting rib pattern.

A word about color: You may knit this tuque in whatever colors you wish, but if you're knitting for a sports-loving recipient, choose wisely. In a famous Québécois children's story, "The Hockey Sweater," author Roch Carrier recounts his outrage when, as a child, he was forced to wear a Toronto Maple Leafs sweater, received by mistake as a replacement for his beloved but worn-out Canadiens sweater. To avoid causing such disenchantment when giving your tuque, research team preferences in advance.

Using A and tubular method (see Special Techniques, page 136), CO 108 (120, 132) sts. Place marker (pm) for beg of rnd and join, being careful not to twist sts. Work 1 rnd of K1, P1 Rib.
Establish Rib and Stripe Patterns:
Change to 3x1 Rib and work even in Stripe Sequence until hat measures 5 (5½, 6¼)".

SHAPE CROWN
Dec rnd 1: [K2tog, k1, p1] around—81 (90, 99) sts rem. Work 7 rnds even, working sts as they appear.
Dec rnd 2: [K2tog, p1] around—54 (60, 66) sts rem. Work 5 rnds even.
Dec rnd 3: K1, *slip 1 wyif, p2tog, psso], k1, p1, k1; rep from * to last 5 sts, slip 1 wyif, p2tog, psso, k1, p1—36 (40, 44) sts rem. Work 3 rnds even.
Dec rnd 4: *Ssk, p2tog; rep from * around—18 (20, 22) sts rem. Work 1 rnd. Rep Dec rnd 4 once more—9 (10, 11) sts rem.

FINISHING
Break yarn, leaving a 12" tail. Using yarn needle, thread tail through all sts twice, then draw tight and fasten off securely. Weave in loose ends. Block to finished measurements.

Halter Swimsuit–Style Vest

SIZES
X-Small (Small, Medium, Large,
X-Large, 2X-Large)
Shown in size Small

FINISHED MEASUREMENTS
Chest: 33 (36, 39, 42, 44½, 48)"

YARN
Schoeller + Stahl Merino Stretch
(44% wool / 43% acrylic / 13% Elite;
174 yds / 50 g): 4 (4, 4, 5, 5, 5) balls
#1322 olive (MC); 1 (1, 1, 2, 2, 2)
ball(s) #1321 natural (A) and 2 (2, 2,
3, 3, 3) balls #1317 turquoise (B)

NEEDLES
One pair 32" circular needles size
US 6 (4 mm)
Change needle size if necessary to
obtain correct gauge.

NOTIONS
Stitch holders, stitch markers,
yarn needle

GAUGE
22 sts and 31 rows = 4" (10 cm) in
Stockinette stitch (St st)

STRIPE PATTERN
Working in St st, work 2 rows A,
2 rows MC, 6 rows B, 2 rows MC,
4 rows A.

NOTE
▸ Although this project is knit flat, a
circular needle is needed to a
ccommodate the large numbers of
stitches for the neck band.

As impractical as they may seem today, hand-knit women's bathing suits of the 1920s were quite a leap forward compared to 19th-century bathing gowns—long dresses in figure-concealing fabrics weighted so they would not rise up in the water. These were donned in bathing machines, horse-drawn cabins rolled out to sea to allow bathers to change and enter the water while staying concealed from the opposite sex. Early the next century, the two-piece suit was adopted, but it still covered the body from shoulder to ankle.

By the 1920s, however, to the alarm of fashion conservatives, body-hugging wool jersey bathing suits had become common, partly in response to women's desire to be more active in water sports. Knitted suits have been popular periodically since that time, particularly during the 1970s. Unfortunately, these suits often prove more useful dry than wet, due to their tendency to lose elasticity in water. With this in mind, I decided on a "dry" vest modeled on the slim fit and halter shaping of 1930s knitted bathing costumes, the first garments to feature the stylistic lines and characteristics of the modern bathing suit.

BACK
With MC, CO 93 (101, 109, 117, 125, 133) sts.
Establish Ribbing: (RS) K2, *p1, k3; rep from * to last 3 sts, end p1, k2. Cont in P1, K3 Rib as est for ¾", ending with a WS row. Work 2 rows in St st.
Work Stripe Pattern and Shape Waist: (RS) Change to A and work Rows 1–16 of Stripe Patt once. AT THE SAME TIME, dec 1 st at each edge on first row, then every other row 8 more times as follows: K2, ssk, knit to last 4 sts, k2tog, k2—75 (83, 91, 99, 107, 115) sts rem. Work even in St st for 6 rows. Inc 1 st each edge on next row, then every 8 rows 1 (2, 3, 4, 5, 6) time(s), and every 6 rows 7 (6, 5, 4, 3, 2) times as follows: K2, M1-R, knit to last 2 sts, M1-L, k2—93 (101, 109, 117, 125, 133) sts. Work even until Back measures 11½ (11¾, 12, 12¼, 12½, 12¾)" ending with a WS row. Place sts on holder.

FRONT
Work as for Back until piece measures 9½ (9¾, 10, 10¼, 10½, 10¾)", ending with a WS row.
Establish Intarsia Pattern: (RS) With MC, k46 (50, 54, 58, 62, 66), join in A and k1, join second ball of MC, knit to end. Cont working Chart, joining B on Row 5 (see Chart Note for continuing Intarsia patt). Work even until Front measures same as Back, ending with a WS row.
Shape Underarms: (RS) BO 6 (8, 19, 12, 14, 16) sts at beg of next 2 rows—81 (85, 89, 93, 97, 101) sts rem.

Next row (RS): K2, k2tog, k32 (34, 36, 38, 40, 42), ssk, k2; BO center st; k2, k2tog, knit to last 4 sts, ssk, k2. Place left neck sts on holder and cont with right neck.

Shape Right Neck:

Row 1 (WS): Purl to last 4 sts, p2tog, p2.

Row 2: K2, k2tog, knit to last 4 sts, ssk, k2. Rep Rows 1–2 9 (10, 11, 11, 12, 14) times, Row 1 0 (1, 1, 0, 1, 0) time, and Row 2 1 (0, 0, 1, 0, 0) time—6 sts rem.

Next RS row: K1, k2tog, ssk, k1—4 sts rem. Purl 1 row.

Next row: K1, ssk, k1. Cut yarn, thread through rem sts, and pull tight.

Shape Left Neck:

Slip left neck sts from holder to needle.

Row 1 (WS): P2, ssp, purl to end.

Row 2: K2, k2tog, knit to last 4 sts, ssk, k2. Rep these 2 rows until 6 sts rem.

Next RS row: K1, k2tog, ssk, k1—4 sts rem. Purl 1 row.

Next row: k1, ssk, k1. Cut yarn, thread through rem sts, and pull tight.

FINISHING

Neck Band: (RS) CO 77 (79, 81, 83, 85, 87) sts, pick up and knit 22 (24, 26, 28, 30, 32) sts along left neck edge, pm for center, pick up and knit 22 (24, 26, 28, 30, 32) sts along right neck edge, CO 77 (79, 81, 83, 85, 87) sts—198 (206, 214, 222, 230, 238) sts. Knit 1 row.

Establish Ribbing: (RS) *P2, k2; rep from * to 3 sts before marker, p1, k2tog, sm; ssk, p1, *k2, p2; rep from * to end. Work 1 row even in Rib as est. Rep these 2 rows once more—194 (202, 210, 218, 226, 234) sts rem. BO all sts.

Sew side seams.

Back Band: (RS) Beg at end of right neck band, pick up and knit 78 (80, 82, 84, 86, 88) sts along cast-on edge of band, 91 (99, 107, 115, 123, 131) sts along Back and 78 (80, 82, 84, 86, 88) sts along cast-on edge of left band—247 (259, 271, 283, 295, 307) sts. Knit 1 row, then work K2, P2 Rib for 4 rows. BO all sts loosely in Rib.

Weave in loose ends. Block to finished measurements.

INTARSIA CHART

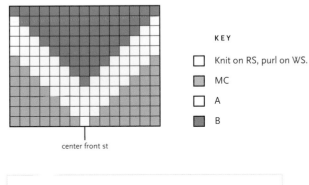

center front st

KEY

☐ Knit on RS, purl on WS.

▦ MC

☐ A

▦ B

CHART NOTE
Intarsia Chart sets up slanting color pattern. Continue shifting colors 1 st to the right on right neck edge and 1 st to the left on left neck edge until only B remains; continue with B only (see photo).

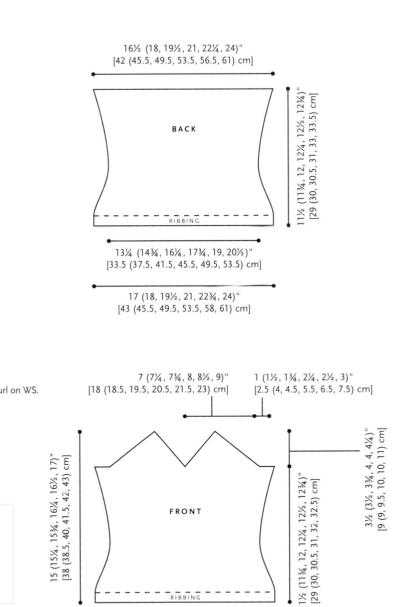

16½ (18, 19½, 21, 22¼, 24)"
[42 (45.5, 49.5, 53.5, 56.5, 61) cm]

BACK

11½ (11¾, 12, 12¼, 12½, 12¾)"
[29 (30, 30.5, 31, 33, 33.5) cm]

RIBBING

13¼ (14¾, 16¼, 17¾, 19, 20½)"
[33.5 (37.5, 41.5, 45.5, 49.5, 53.5) cm]

17 (18, 19½, 21, 22¾, 24)"
[43 (45.5, 49.5, 53.5, 58, 61) cm]

7 (7¼, 7¾, 8, 8½, 9)"
[18 (18.5, 19.5, 20.5, 21.5, 23) cm]

1 (1½, 1¾, 2¼, 2½, 3)"
[2.5 (4, 4.5, 5.5, 6.5, 7.5) cm]

FRONT

15 (15¼, 15¾, 16¼, 16½, 17)"
[38 (38.5, 40, 41.5, 42, 43) cm]

11½ (11¾, 12, 12¼, 12½, 12¾)"
[29 (30, 30.5, 31, 32, 32.5) cm]

3½ (3½, 3¾, 4, 4, 4¼)"
[9 (9, 9.5, 10, 10, 11) cm]

RIBBING

SPECIAL TECHNIQUES

Backward Loop CO: Make a loop (using a slip knot) with the working yarn and place it on the needle [first st CO], * wind yarn around left thumb clockwise, insert right-hand needle into the front of the loop on thumb, remove thumb and tighten st on needle; repeat from * for remaining sts to be CO, or for casting on at the end of a row in progress.

Centering Color Patterns: Centering color patterns on a pattern piece is the same whether the piece is knit flat or in the round; the number of stitches on the needles must be counted and divided by the number of stitches in the pattern repeat and the balancing stitch(es), if applicable.

When balancing stitch(es) are present
Balancing stitches are extra stitches which are not repeated; they are added to keep the pattern repeat symmetrical. In the written-out version of a pattern, the repeat and balancing stitches are included in parentheses (e.g., "multiple of 8 sts + 1" is an 8-stitch pattern repeat with 1 balancing stitch); in the charted version of a pattern, the repeat is indicated at the bottom and the balancing stitches fall outside of the marked repeat.

1. Subtract the balancing stitches from the total number of stitches on the needles. 125 is used as the example for this demonstration as the number of stitches over which to center the pattern repeat: 125−1=124.
2. Divide the result in half: 124/2 = 62 stitches.
3. This last number is divided once again, this time by the number of stitches present in the repeat/multiple: 62/8=7.75. Had this been a whole number, no further calculations would be needed—just begin knitting the first stitch of the repeat. Since it isn't, go on to Step 4.
4. Multiply the number of complete repeats (7) by the number of stitches in the repeat (8): 7 x 8 = 56.

5. Subtract the number from Step 4 from the number from Step 2: 62 − 56 = 6.
6. Subtract the number from Step 5 from the number of stitches in the stitch repeat: 8 − 6 = 2.
7. Exclude the number from Step 6 in the first repeat worked, i.e., begin on the third stitch of the repeat and continue normally.

Check your work midway though the first row; if the balancing stitch is in the center, all is well.

Whole repeats only

When a repeat doesn't need to be completed to be symmetrical, there are no "balancing stitches" included. Generally, this occurs when working a pattern with an even number of stitches—the total stitch count will also be an even number.

1. Divide the number of stitches on the needles by the number of stitches in the repeat—for example, if you have 124 stitches on your needles with an 8-stitch repeat, 124/8 = 15.5. As in the previous example, had the resulting number been a whole number, no further calculations would be needed—just begin knitting the first stitch of the repeat. Since it isn't, go on to Step 2.
2. Multiply the number of complete repeats (15) by the number of stitches in the repeat (8): 15 x 8 = 120.
3. Subtract the number from Step 2 from the number of stitches on the needles: 124 − 120 = 4.
4. Divide the number from Step 3 in half: 4/2 = 2
5. Exclude the number from Step 4 in the first repeat worked, i.e., begin on the third stitch of the repeat and continue normally.

When knitting, check that an entire repeat has been worked when half the stitches have been knit. If that is the case, continue normally.

Crochet Chain: Make a slipknot and place on hook, * yarn over and draw through loop on hook; repeat from * for desired length.

Duplicate Stitch: Duplicate st is similar to Kitchener st, except it is used for decorative purposes instead of joining two pieces together. Thread a yarn needle with chosen yarn (leaving a tail to be woven in later); *bring the needle from WS to RS of work at the base of the st to be covered, pass the needle under both loops above the st to be covered (the base of the st above); insert the needle into the same place where you started (base of st), and pull yarn through to WS of work. Be sure that the new st is the same tension as the rest of the piece. Repeat from * for additional sts.

A good way to visualize the path of the yarn for Duplicate st is to work a swatch in Stockinette st using main color (MC) for three rows, work 1 row alternating MC and a contrasting color, then work two additional rows using MC only.

Garter Stitch: Knit every row when working back and forth; knit 1 round, purl 1 round when working in the round.

I-Cord: Using a double-pointed needle, cast on or pick up the required number of sts; the working yarn will be at the left-hand side of the needle. *Transfer the needle with the sts to your left hand, bring the yarn around behind the work to the right-hand side; using a second double-pointed needle, knit the sts from right to left, pulling the yarn from left to right for the first st; do not turn. Slide the sts to the opposite end of the needle; repeat from * until the cord is the length desired. Note: After a few rows, the tubular shape will become apparent.

Intarsia Colorwork Method: Use a separate length of yarn for each color section; you may wind yarn onto bobbins to make color changes easier. When changing colors, bring the new yarn up and to the right of the yarn just used to interlock the yarns and prevent leaving a hole; do not carry colors not in use across the back of the work.

Kitchener Stitch: Using a blunt yarn needle, thread a length of yarn approximately 4 times the length of the section to be joined. Hold the pieces to be joined with wrong sides together and with the needles holding the sts parallel, both ends pointing in the same direction. Working from right to left, insert yarn needle into first st on front needle as if to purl, and pull yarn through, leaving st on needle; insert yarn needle into first st on back needle as if to knit, and pull yarn through, leaving st on needle; *insert yarn needle into first st on front needle as if to knit, pull yarn through, remove st from needle; insert yarn needle into next st on front needle as if to purl, pull yarn through, leave st on needle; insert yarn needle into first st on back needle as if to purl, pull yarn through, remove st from needle; insert yarn needle into next st on back needle as if to knit, pull yarn through, leave st on needle. Repeat from *, working 3 or 4 sts at a time, then go back and adjust tension to match the pieces being joined. When 1 st remains on each needle, cut yarn and pass through last 2 sts to fasten off.

Long-tail CO: Leaving tail with about 1" of yarn for each st to be cast-on, make a slipknot in the yarn and place it on the right-hand needle. Insert the thumb and forefinger of your left hand between the strands of yarn so that the working end is around your forefinger, and the tail end is around your thumb 'slingshot' fashion; *insert the tip of the right-hand needle into the front loop on the thumb, hook the strand of yarn coming from the forefinger from back to front, and draw it through the loop on your thumb; remove your thumb from the loop and pull on the working yarn to tighten the new st on

the right-hand needle; return your thumb and forefinger to their original positions, and repeat from * for remaining sts to be CO.

Pompom: You can use a pompom maker or the following method: Cut two cardboard circles in the diameter of the pompom desired. Cut a 1" diameter hole in the center of each circle. Cut away a small wedge out of each circle to allow for wrapping yarn. Hold the circles together with the openings aligned. Wrap yarn around the circles until there is no room left in the center to wrap. Carefully cut yarn around outer edge of the cardboard circles. Using a 12" length of yarn, wrap around strands between the two circles and tie tightly. Slip the cardboard circles off the completed pompom; trim pompom, leaving the ends of the tie untrimmed. Using ends of tie, sew pompom to garment.

Provisional CO: Using waste yarn, CO the required number of sts; work in Stockinette st for 3-4 rows; work 1 row with a thin, smooth yarn, (crochet cotton or ravel cord used for machine knitting), as a separator; change to main yarn and continue as directed. When ready to work the live sts, pull out the separator row, placing the live sts on a spare needle.

Provisional (Crochet Chain) CO: Using a crochet hook and smooth yarn, (crochet cotton or ravel cord used for machine knitting), work a crochet chain with a few more chains than the number of sts needed; fasten off. If desired, tie a knot on the fastened-off end to mark the end that you will be unraveling from later. Turn the chain over; with a needle 1 size smaller than required for piece and working yarn, and starting a few chains in from the beginning of the chain, pick up and knit one st in each bump at the back of the chain, leaving any extra chains at the end unworked.

Change to needle size required for project on first row.

When ready to work the live sts, unravel the chain by loosening the fastened-off end and 'unzipping' the chain, placing the live sts on a spare needle.

Reading Charts: Unless otherwise specified in the instructions, when working back and forth, charts are read from right to left for RS rows, and left to right for WS rows. Row numbers are written at the beginning of each row. Numbers on the right indicate RS rows; numbers on the left indicate WS rows. When working in the round, all rounds are read from right to left.

Sewn BO: Break off yarn, leaving a long tail (approximately 12" for every 10 sts to be BO); thread tail onto yarn needle. With RS facing, tail at left and above work, * insert needle into second st from left as if to knit and into first st as if to purl; pull yarn through and slip first st off the needle. Repeat from * until all sts have been bound off, keeping the tension fairly loose; it may be tightened later.

Short Row Shaping (wrap and turn method): Work the number of sts specified in the instructions, wrap and turn [wrp-t] as follows:

Bring yarn to the front (purl position), slip the next st to the right-hand needle, bring yarn to back of work, return slipped st on right hand needle to left-hand needle; turn, ready to work the next row, leaving remaining sts unworked.

When Short Rows are completed, or when working progressively longer Short Rows, work the wrap together with the wrapped st as you come to it as follows:

If st is to be worked as a knit st, insert the right-hand needle into the wrap from below, then into the wrapped st, and k2tog; if st to be worked is a purl st, insert needle into the wrapped st, then down into the wrap, and p2tog. (Wrap may be lifted onto the left-hand needle, then worked together with the wrapped st if this is easier.)

Short Row Shaping (yarnover method): Instead of wrapping stitches as above, work a yarnover after the turn. Join the Short Rows as instructed in the pattern.

Steek: A steek is a field of extra stitches that is inserted when working Stranded (Fair Isle) style in the round; it will be cut after the piece is finished, e.g., for the front of a cardigan. These stitches are not usually included in the stitch count. Work and cut as instructed in the text. When picking up stitches after cutting a steek, pick up between the last (first) steek stitch and the first (last) pattern stitch; the steek stitches will turn to the WS. To finish, trim the steek sts and whipstitch to WS.

Stranded (Fair Isle) Colorwork Method: When more than one color is used per row, carry color(s) not in use loosely across the WS of work. Be sure to secure all colors at beginning and end of rows to prevent holes.

3-Needle BO: Place the sts to be joined onto two same-size needles; hold the pieces to be joined with the right sides facing each other and the needles parallel, both pointing to the right. Holding both needles in your left hand, using working yarn and a third needle same size or one size larger, insert third needle into first st on front needle, then into first st on back needle; knit these 2 sts together; *knit next st from each needle together (2 sts on right-hand needle); pass first st over second st to BO one st. Repeat from * until one st remains on third needle; cut yarn and fasten off.

Tubular BO: This BO often requires 2 or more rows of Tubular Stockinette st (Tubular St st) before working the actual BO; the edge will be firmer if Tubular St st is done with needles 1 or 2 sizes smaller than size used for ribbing. Work 3 to 5 rows [rnds] in Tubular St st (see below), unless instructed otherwise.

Cut yarn leaving a tail about 4 times the length of edge to be BO (if a large area is to be grafted and the yarn is inclined to fray, it may be necessary to do this in small sections, weaving ends in on wrong side as you go).

Thread tail on a yarn needle. As you work, do not pull the yarn too tightly; try to match the tension of the rest of the knitting; work 3 or 4 sts, then go back and adjust tension if necessary; * insert yarn needle into first st on the left-hand needle as if to knit, and remove it from the needle; insert yarn needle as if to purl in the front of work into the third st (now the second st remaining on the left-hand needle), and pull yarn through; insert yarn needle as if to purl into the second st (now the first st remaining on the left-hand needle), and remove it from the needle; working around the back of the third st (now the first st on the left-hand needle); insert the yarn needle into the fourth st (now the second st on the left-hand needle) as if to knit, and pull the yarn through. Repeat from * until you have BO all sts; pull tail through the remaining st and fasten off.

Tubular CO: This CO often requires 2 or more rows of Tubular Stockinette st (Tubular St st) after the CO and before beginning the ribbing; the edge will be firmer if Tubular St st is done with needles 1 or 2 sizes smaller than size to be used for ribbing. Using ribbing size needles, waste yarn, and using Backwards Loop CO, CO half the number of sts required (plus 1 if an odd number of sts is required); [if desired, knit 1 row with crochet cotton or ravel cord to make it easier to remove waste yarn later]; break yarn. Using larger needles and working yarn, [k1, p1] in each st [or *k1, yo; rep from * across], doubling the number of sts. NOTE: If you require an odd number of sts and are working back and forth, knit the last st (DO NOT double it). If you are working in the round, double the st; you will need to decrease 1 st on the first row after ribbing to return to an odd number of sts.

Work per instructions or work Tubular St st (see below) for 2–4 rows.

Change to ribbing size needles and work for length desired in 1x1 ribbing, or as instructed in the pattern. Remove waste yarn from beginning by pulling ravel cord, or unravel waste yarn.

Tubular Stockinette Stitch (Tubular St st): Two or more rows [rnds] of Tubular St st are often required after working Tubular CO or before working Tubular BO. For working back and forth: Row 1: * K1, slip 1 wyif; rep from * across (end k1 if an odd number of sts). Row 2: (Slip 1 wyif if an odd number of sts) * K1, slip 1 wyif; rep from * across. For working in-the-round: Rnd 1: * K1, slip 1 wyif; rep from * around. Rnd 2: * Slip 1 wyib, p1; rep from * around. Repeat Rows [Rnds] 1 and 2 as specified in the pattern. NOTE: If working before Tubular BO and after 1 or more rows of 1x1 rib, you will be knitting the knit sts and slipping the purl sts on every row.

Twisted Cord: Fold one strand (or number of strands specified in the pattern) in half and secure one end to a stationary object. Twist from other end until it begins to buckle. Fold twisted length in half and holding ends together, allow to twist up on itself. Tie end in an overhand knot to secure.

Yarnover (yo): Bring yarn forward (to the purl position), then place it in position to work the next st. If next st is to be knit, bring yarn over the needle and knit; if next st is to be purled, bring yarn over the needle and then forward again to the purl position and purl. Work the yarnover in pattern on the next row unless instructed otherwise.

approx = approximately

beg = begin/beginning

BO = bind off

CC = contrast color

ch = chain stitch

cm = centimeter(s)

cn = cable needle

CO = cast on

cont = continue/continuing

dec = decrease/decreases/decreasing

dpn(s) = double-pointed needle(s)

est = established

g = gram

inc = increase

k = knit

k1-tbl = Knit one st through the back loop, twisting the st.

k2tog = Knit 2 sts together

k3tog = Knit 3 sts together

LH = left-hand

m = meter(s)

M1 or M1-L (make 1-left slanting) = With the tip of the left-hand needle inserted from front to back, lift the strand between the two needles onto the left-hand needle; knit the strand through the back loop to increase one st.

M1-R (make 1-right slanting) = With the tip of the left-hand needle inserted from back to front, lift the strand between the two needles onto the left-hand needle; knit it through the front loop to increase one st.

M1P (make 1 purlwise) = With the tip of the left-hand needle inserted from back to front, lift the strand between the two needles onto the left-hand needle; purl the strand through the front loop to increase one st.

MC = main color

mm = millimeter(s)

N1, N2, N3, N4 = Needles 1, 2, 3, 4

oz = ounce(s)

p = purl

patt(s) = pattern(s)

pm = Place marker

p2tog = Purl 2 sts together

psso (pass slipped stitch over) = Pass slipped st on right-hand needle of the st(s) indicated in the instructions, as in binding off.

rem = remain(ing)

rep = repeat(s)

Rev St st = Reverse Stockinette stitch. Purl on RS rows, knit on WS rows when working back and forth; purl every rnd when working in the round.

RH = right-hand

rm = remove marker

rnd(s) = round(s)

RS = right side

sc (single crochet) = Insert hook into next st and draw up a loop (2 loops on hook), yarnover and draw through both loops on hook.

sk2p (double decrease) = Slip next st knitwise to right-hand needle, k2tog, pass slipped st over st from k2tog.

sm = Slip marker

ssk (slip, slip, knit; left-leaning double decrease) = Slip the next 2 sts to the right-hand needle one at a time as if to knit; return them back to left-hand needle one at a time in their new orientation; knit them together through the back loops.

sssk (slip, slip, slip, knit; left-leaning triple decrease) = Slip the next 3 sts to the right needle one at a time as if to knit; return them to the left needle one at a time in their new orientation; knit them together through the back loop.

ssp (slip, slip, purl; left-leaning double decrease) = Slip the next 2 sts to right-hand needle one at a time as if to knit; return them to the left-hand needle one at a time in their new orientation; purl them together through the back loops.

st(s) = stitch(es)

St st = Stockinette stitch/Stocking stitch. Knit on RS rows, purl on WS rows when working back and forth; knit every round when working in the round.

tbl = through back loop

tog = together

WS = wrong side

wrp-t = Wrap and turn (see Special Techniques—Short Row Shaping)

wyib = with yarn in back

wyif = with yarn in front

yd(s) = yard(s)

yfwd = yarn forward

yo = yarnover (see Special Techniques)

[ ] = Work instructions within brackets as many times as directed

( ) = Instructions are given for smallest size, with larger sizes inside parentheses. When only 1 number is given, it applies to all sizes. Also used for work to be done within a single stitch.

✳ = Repeat instructions following the single asterisk as directed

" = inch(es)

**Adrienne Vittadini /
Grignasco / Jo Sharp/
Reynolds**
JCA Inc.
35 Scales Lane
Townsend, MA 01469
978-597-8794

AmiAmi
35 Wilshire
Hudson, Quebec J0P 1H0
Canada
www.ami-itoya.com/ca

Blue Sky Alpacas, Inc.
PO Box 387
St. Francis, MN 55070
888-460-8862
www.blueskyalpacas.com

Brown Sheep Company, Inc.
100662 County Road 16
Mitchell, NE 69357
800-826-9136
www.brownsheep.com

Cascade Yarns
1224 Andover Park East
Tukwila, WA 98188
800-548-1048
www.cascadeyarns.com

Classic Elite Yarns
122 Western Avenue
Lowell, MA 01851
800-343-0308
www.classiceliteyarns.com

Dale of Norway, Inc.
4750 Shelburne Road
Suite 20
Shelburne, VT 05482
262-544-1996
www.dale.no

GGH /Muench Yarns
1323 Scott Street
Petaluma, CA 94954
800-733-9276
www.muenchyarns.com

Jamieson & Smith Yarns
Dist. by Wheelsmith Wools
308 S. Pennsylvania Avenue
Centre Hall, PA 16828
877-474-0026
www.wheelsmithwools.com

La Lana Wools
136-C Paseo Norte
Taos, NM 87571
505-758-9631
www.lalanawools.com

Louet Sales
808 Commerce Park Drive
Ogdensburg, NY 13669
613-925-4502
www.louet.com

Mountain Colors
PO Box 156
Corvallis, MT 59828
406-961-1900
www.mountaincolors.com

Needful Yarns Inc.
4476 Chesswood Drive
Toronto, ON M3J2B9
Canada
OR
60 Industrial Pkwy. PMB #233
Cheektowaga, NY 14227
866-800-4700
www.needfulyarnsinc.com

Patons Yarns Inc.
320 Livingstone Avenue South
Listowel, ON N4W 3H3
Canada
888-368-8401
www.patonsyarns.com

Plymouth Yarn Company
PO Box 28
Bristol, PA 19007
215-788-0459
www.plymouthyarn.com

Rowan
Dist. by Westminster Fibers
4 Townsend West, Unit 8
Nashua, NH 03063
603-886-5041
www.knitrowan.com

Schachenmayr Yarns
Dist. by Knitting Fever
35 Debevoise Ave.
Roosevelt, NY 11575
800-645-3457
www.knittingfever.com

Skacel Collection Inc.
PO Box 88110
Seattle, WA 98138-2110
425-291-9600
www.skacelknitting.com

SELECTED BIBLIOGRAPHY

FASHION — SOCIAL AND HISTORICAL STUDIES

Hollander, Anne, *Feeding the Eye*, Farrar, Straus and Giroux, 1999

Hollander, Anne, *Sex and Suits*, Alfred A. Knopf, 1994

Polhemus, Ted, *Style Surfing: What to Wear in the 3rd Millennium*, Thames & Hudson, 1996

Polhemus, Ted, *Streetstyle: From Sidewalk to Catwalk*, Thames & Hudson, 1994

Rubinstein, Ruth P., *Dress Codes: Meanings and Messages in American Culture*, Westview Press, 1995

Weissman Joselit, Jenna, *A Perfect Fit: Clothes, Character, and the Promise of America*, Rept. Owl Books, 2002

FASHION — ART & PHOTOGRAPHY (coffee table books)

De La Haye, Amy, *The Cutting Edge,* The Overlook Press, 1997

De La Haye, Amy and Shelley Tobin, *Chanel: the Couturière at Work,* V & A Publications, 1994

De La Haye, Amy, *Fashion Sourcebook*, Time Warner Books UK, 1988

Kirke, Betty, *Madeleine Vionnet*, Chronicle Books, 1998

Kyoto Costume Institute, *Fashion,* Taschen, 2002

McDowell, Colin, *The Man of Fashion: Peacock Males and Perfect Gentlemen*, Thames and Hudson, 1997

Milbank, Caroline Rennolds, *New York Fashion: The Evolution of American Style*, Harry N. Abrams, 1988

Roetzel, Bernhard, *Gentleman: A Timeless Fashion*, Könemann, 2004

Various. *Key Moments in Fashion,* Hamlyn, 1998

KNITTING — REFERENCE

Stanley, Montse, *Knitter's Handbook*, Reader's Digest, 1993

Thomas, Mary, *Mary Thomas's Knitting Book*, Rept. Dover, 1972

Thomas, Mary, *Mary Thomas's Book of Knitting Patterns*, Rept. Dover, 1972

Walker, Barbara, *Treasuries of Knitting Patterns Vols 1–4*, Rept. Schoolhouse Press, 1998–2000

Zimmermann, Elizabeth, *Knitting Without Tears*, Fireside, 1973

KNITTING — HISTORICAL REPRODUCTIONS

Weldon's Practical Needlework Vols 1–12, Rept. Interweave Press, 1999–2005

Kliot, Jules & Kaethe, editors, *Knitting: 19th Century Sources*, Lacis, 1998

1891 The Art of Knitting, Piper Publishing, 2004

Fleisher's Knitting & Crocheting Manual 8th Edition, Iva Rose Vintage Reproductions, 2005

Fleisher's Knitting & Crocheting Manual 19th Edition, Iva Rose Vintage Reproductions, 2005

KNITTING — HISTORY

MacDonald, Anne L., *No Idle Hands*, Ballantine, 1988

Rutt, Richard, *A History of Handknitting*, B. T. Batsford, 1987

Scott, Shirley, *Canada Knits*, McGraw-Hill Ryerson, 1990

KNITTING — REGIONAL HISTORY & PATTERNS

Brown-Reinsel, Beth, *Knitting Ganseys,* Interweave Press, 1993

Bush, Nancy, *Folk Socks*, Interweave Press, 1994

Gibson-Roberts, Priscilla A., *Ethnic Socks & Stockings*, XRX, 1995

Khmeleva, Galina and Carol R. Noble, *Gossamer Webs*, Interweave Press, 1998

Lind, Vibeke, *Knitting in the Nordic Tradition*, Rept. Lark, 1992

McGregor, Sheila, *Traditional Fair Isle Knitting*, Rept. Dover, 2003

Pagoldh, Susanne, *Nordic Knitting*, Rept. Interweave Press, 1997

Sundbo, Annemor, *Setesdal Sweaters*, Torridals Tweed, 2001

Thompson, Gladys, *Patterns for Guernseys, Jerseys & Arans*, Rept. Dover, 1971

Upitis, Lizbeth, *Latvian Mittens*, Rept. Schoolhouse Press, 1997

ACKNOWLEDGMENTS

While I'm named as the sole author of this book, many have assisted me in bringing it to fruition. I'd like first to thank Melanie Falick and Pam Allen, the former my editor at Stewart, Tabori & Chang, and the latter the editor of *Interweave Knits;* their exemplary work inspired me long before I could call myself a designer, and I am fortunate to be able to count them as friends. I'm also indebted to Alan Getz, who allowed me to assume the position of creative director at JCA while I was working on this book. Holding this position has been a dream come true, and coworkers Jill Giard, Barbara Khouri, and the rest of the JCA team make it so.

Thanks also go out to my technical editor, Charlotte Quiggle, whose keen eye and intelligent approach are equal only to her designing skills, to Sue McCain, whose technical illustrations and charts grace these pages, and to Susi Oberhelman, for sharing her elegant graphic design.

The photo shoots were a true team effort, and I don't think any of it could have been done without Mary Jackson, who tirelessly toiled at completing our team, finding models, organizing every aspect, and keeping everyone happy through it all. Photographer Sara Cameron brought her artistic vision to the mix, while make-up artists Nathalie Lachance and Amélie Thomas beautified our team of charming models: Andreas Apergis, Sean Butler, Melissa Carrière Charles, Emma Davida Catmur, Valérie Duemié, Marcel Jeannin, David Leblanc, Melanie Martens, Hisako Mori, Lesley Phord-Toy, France Rolland, Jenny Adams, Anana Rydvald, Millie Tresierra, Oona, and Zoe.

I wasn't born in Montreal and only moved here as an adult, but I love it as if it were my hometown. The photographs were taken in some of the city's most distinctive locations: Mont Royal, Old Montreal, Java U Café (www.java-u.com), and the historic Monument National (www.monument-national.qc.ca). I'd like to thank Richard M. Dumont and Claudia Besso for welcoming us into their home, as well as Marco at Java U and Anne-Marie Bonin at the Monument National.

I am also grateful to all the talented knitters who helped me knit samples—Mona Schmidt, my associate at JCA, laid her own knitting aside more often than I can count, and was joined by Molly Ann Rothschild, Mireille Holland, Fran Scullin, and Lucinda Heller. Friends came to the rescue as the end drew near and helped finish things, all the while keeping my spirits high: Mona, Molly Ann, Emma, Melanie, Nathalie, and Mary. The entire Montreal Knits gang (www.montrealknits.blog-city.com) could also always be counted on for company, no matter the weather.

But most importantly of all, I would like to thank my husband, Marcel Jeannin, and my daughter, Oona. Their love and support have meant more than I can describe in mere words, and I plan on dedicating a lot more time to them now that this book is finished.

INDEX

ABOUT THE AUTHOR

VÉRONIK AVERY

Véronik Avery lives in Montreal, where she serves as creative director for JCA Yarns. She is a regular contributor to *Interweave Knits* magazine. Her work has also appeared in the books *Weekend Knitting, Handknit Holidays, Knit Wit, Wrap Style*, and *Folk Style*, and the magazine *Woman's Day*. This is her first book.